How Regions Grow

TRENDS AND ANALYSIS

OECD

ORGANISATION FOR ECONOMIC CO-OPERATION AND DEVELOPMENT

The OECD is a unique forum where the governments of 30 democracies work together to address the economic, social and environmental challenges of globalisation. The OECD is also at the forefront of efforts to understand and to help governments respond to new developments and concerns, such as corporate governance, the information economy and the challenges of an ageing population. The Organisation provides a setting where governments can compare policy experiences, seek answers to common problems, identify good practice and work to co-ordinate domestic and international policies.

The OECD member countries are: Australia, Austria, Belgium, Canada, the Czech Republic, Denmark, Finland, France, Germany, Greece, Hungary, Iceland, Ireland, Italy, Japan, Korea, Luxembourg, Mexico, the Netherlands, New Zealand, Norway, Poland, Portugal, the Slovak Republic, Spain, Sweden, Switzerland, Turkey, the United Kingdom and the United States. The Commission of the European Communities takes part in the work of the OECD.

OECD Publishing disseminates widely the results of the Organisation's statistics gathering and research on economic, social and environmental issues, as well as the conventions, guidelines and standards agreed by its members.

This work is published on the responsibility of the Secretary-General of the OECD. The opinions expressed and arguments employed herein do not necessarily reflect the official views of the Organisation or of the governments of its member countries.

Also available in French under the title:
Régions et croissance : Une analyse des tendances

Foreword

Globalisation in the OECD has come to regions more strongly than to nations. Technological change and the gradual reduction of the working age population are two main challenges influencing the economic performance of many regions. While some regions are able to adapt to these challenges and reap the benefits of globalisation, others remain stagnant and struggle to compete in the global arena.

Technological change has led to the rapid growth of service industries and the knowledge-based economy, allowing those regions specialised in the production of information and knowledge to become more competitive in the global economy. Nonetheless a region's capacity to innovate is not its only source of growth; equally important is its ability to create a high-quality population, to retain and attract talented people, to be well connected to global markets, to have an adequate business environment and infrastructure system and a well-functioning labour market.

These challenges coincide with an increasing concentration of economic activity. People and firms are increasingly concentrating geographically, driven by the benefits of economies of agglomeration. But the concentration of economic activity and people has both positive (growth spurred by higher productivity levels and innovation) and negative outcomes (inequality between regions).

Under these conditions, we need to understand regional competitiveness better and to decide on the best policy responses. The OECD created the Territorial Development Policy Committee (TDPC) in 1999 as a unique forum for international exchange and debate. It also formed the Working Party for Territorial Indicators (WPTI) to carry out statistical work on the measurement of regional economies.

This publication, How Regions Grow: Trends and Analysis, aims to measure the overall trends in economic performance and inequality in OECD regions, and to identify the main determinants of regional competitiveness. The book is organised into three main chapters: i) Overall growth trends; ii) Analysing the components of GDP growth; and iii) Assessing the impact of the main determinants of regional growth: a parametric analysis.

The first chapter measures overall growth trends in GDP, GDP per capita and GDP per worker among all OECD regions, within OECD countries, and among predominantly urban, intermediate and predominantly rural regions. The second chapter applies an accounting framework to break GDP growth down into six factors, *allowing us to identify the components of the success of certain regions and to perceive the existence of untapped resources in others.*

Finally, the third chapter uses a series of econometric models to measure both the trends (convergence or divergence) in economic growth and the determinants of such performance.

Acknowledgements

T his report was elaborated by the Regional Competitiveness and Governance Division from the Directorate of Public Governance and Territorial Development (GOV/RCG) of the OECD. The process that led to the final version of the report was directed by Mario Pezzini and co-ordinated by Enrique Garcilazo. It included presenting each individual chapter to the Working Party on Territorial Indicators (WPTI) and to the Territorial Development Policy Committee (TDCP), where useful input and suggestions led to subsequent revisions of the manuscript.

The report was drafted and co-ordinated by Enrique Garcilazo and co-authored by Javier Sanchez-Reaza, with contributions from other OECD Secretariat members including Brunella Boselli, Monica Brezzi, David Freshwater, Nick Vanston, Mauro Migotto, Vicente Ruiz and Vincenzo Spiezia. Very valuable suggestions and input were given by Ray Bollman (Statistics Canada), John Prodromos-Ioannis Prodromidis (KEPE, Greece), Lewis Dijkstra (DG Regio, European Commission), William Kittredge (Economic Development Agency, United States), Andrés Rodríguez-Pose (London School of Economics) and Dev Virdee (Office of National Statistics, United Kingdom).

Ms. Jeanette Duboys and Ms. Sophia Katsira prepared the report for publication and a special thanks to Kate Lancaster for editorial support.

Table of Contents

Figures

ISBN 978-92-64-03945-2
How Regions Grow: Trends and Analysis
© OECD 2009

Acronyms and Abbreviations

TL2	Territorial Level 2
TL3	Territorial Level 3
CRS	Constant returns to scale
GDP	Gross domestic product
IRS	Increasing returns to scale
NEG	New economic geography
OECD	Organisation for Economic Co-operation and Development
OLS	Ordinary least square
pc	Per capita
pp	Percentage points
ppp	Purchasing power parity
PR	Predominantly rural
PU	Predominantly urban
IN	Intermediate
R&D	Research and development
HE	Higher education institutions
BUS	Business sector
GOV	Government sector
PNP	Private non-profit sector
KIS	Knowledge intensive services
HTM	High and medium high-tech manufacturing

ISBN 978-92-64-03945-2
How Regions Grow: Trends and Analysis
© OECD 2009

Executive Summary

Differences across regions within countries are often greater than differences between countries, yet economists, policy makers and international organisations have paid less attention to regional development than national growth. Marked variations in economic performance among OECD regions reflects the regions' great diversity in income levels, employment rates, mixes of high and low productivity activities, assets, comparative advantages, stages of development and public policies.

The current debate on regional policy and development focuses on whether policies should be pro-equity or pro-efficiency, insisting that a trade-off is inevitable. This report departs from this view, emphasising instead that opportunities for growth exist in all regions. It reframes the debate, arguing that national governments should promote growth in *all* regions. And regions should promote their own growth by mobilising local assets and resources so as to capitalise on their specific competitive advantages, rather than depending on national transfers and subsidies to help them grow.

Traditional policies based only on infrastructure provision or schooling are not sufficient for this task; instead a more comprehensive policy is called for, one that integrates these two policies in a co-ordinated agenda across levels government and that foster business development and innovation. This report also shows that innovation and other growth determinants have a very strong geographic – or spatial – dimension that ultimately explains why some regions grow and not others. These efforts are not in detriment of efficiency as comparative advantage and complementarities across regions will ensure that growth in one place produces benefits elsewhere.

This report describes the general trends in regional growth and analyses its key components. It offers:

- An examination of trends in regional GDP, GDP per capita and productivity for two levels of regions within OECD countries for the period 1995-2005.

- An analysis to measure patterns of convergence and divergence that i) compares all OECD regions with each other (international comparison) and ii) compares regions within individual OECD countries (intra-national comparison).

- A development of a regional typology based on average per capita GDP levels and growth rates.

- A breakdown of regional growth into six major components to find patterns among successful and unsuccessful OECD regions.

- Four econometric models to explore trends and regional drivers of growth.

What are the general trends in regional growth?

- **The economic performance of regions varies more than for countries.** GDP, GDP per capita and labour productivity vary more widely across OECD regions than across countries. The disparity in growth among OECD regions exceeded that among countries by almost three times between 1995 and 2005. These wide differences in economic performance highlight the great heterogeneity among OECD regions as a result of differences in their comparative advantages, stages of development and public policies.

- **Rural and urban regions vary significantly in their economic performance and growth is possible in all types of regions.** Although urban regions tend to be richer, well-performing regions – in terms of economic growth – can be found among urban, intermediate and rural regions alike. Indeed, a significant number of urban regions grew faster than rural regions, but also a significant number of rural regions outperformed urban regions. This means that there is no single path to attaining sustainable growth and suggests that there are opportunities for growth in all types of regions.

- **Regional inequality increased between 1995 and 2005 in about 70% of OECD countries.** Only Belgium, France, Germany, Italy, Japan, Mexico, Spain and Turkey reduced disparities among larger regions (known as TL2 regions) and only Austria, Germany, Italy, Japan, Mexico, Spain and Turkey did so among smaller regions (known as TL3 regions). A supplementary analysis over a longer time period (1980-1995) reveals that in approximately one-third of OECD countries regional inequalities declined, in one-third they increased, and in the remaining third there was no clear trend.

- **There is no conclusive evidence that the average GDP per capita of OECD regions began to converge during 1995-2005.** Two complementary analyses reveal no absolute convergence in GDP per capita among TL2 regions between 1995 and 2005. There was some convergence among TL3 regions.

- **Regional convergence during 1995-2005 is only conditional on factors associated with growth.** Convergence among TL2 regions occurs when the analysis accounts for key determinants of regional growth such as innovation, infrastructure and human capital.

- **Convergence is associated with the level of development (*i.e.* GDP per capita).** Richer regions from the bottom quartile of the GDP per capita distribution are growing faster than their counterparts, while poorer regions from the top three quartiles of GDP per capita distribution are growing fastest within their group. Thus, there is some convergence within this subgroup. The analysis in this report cannot differentiate the effects that regional polices (or their absence) have on convergence.

- **Regions with a larger GDP have steadier growth rates than regions with a smaller GDP.** When measured by their GDP share in the OECD, only small regions display annual growth rates above 4% and below 1%. Medium and large regions rarely display negative annual average growth rates.

What are the main components of regional growth?

The components associated with fast-growing regions

- High national growth rates tend to be associated with high regional growth rates. The direction of causation can run either way: Just as national growth can influence regional performance, high regional growth may actually boost national performance. However, national factors are a necessary but not sufficient condition for regional growth.

- High regional growth is also associated with improvements in productivity (defined as average value-added per employed person) and/or with gains in the employment to population ratio (*i.e.* the proportion of the population employed). Therefore, there appears to be no trade-off between productivity and employment among fast-growing regions.

- Labour markets are also important for fast-growing regions, especially when labour supply and labour demand increase simultaneously. Thus we find higher regional growth when the employment rate, the participation rate and the activity rate improve simultaneously.

- High population growth also appears to be common among many of the top-performing regions.

The components associated with slow-growing regions

- Localised factors (productivity, employment rates, participation rates, activity rates and population) seem to play a larger role than national factors in determining the poor performance of regions. More precisely, the 20 slowest-growing regions experienced a contraction in activity rates and loss of efficiency (productivity) rather than a decline in national factors.

- Among the localised factors, regional performance is particularly vulnerable to declines in the employment-to-population ratio, either when it occurs alone or simultaneously with declines in labour productivity. Growth is lowest when both factors decline simultaneously.
- When both labour supply (i.e. participation rates) and labour demand (i.e. employment rates) decline simultaneously growth can be significantly undermined.

The relative importance of national *versus* regional factors

Regional factors are not always correlated with national and common factors: a significant number of regions are either i) improving their overall position in the OECD despite a weak national performance (20 regions); or ii) losing their overall share despite gains in national factors (42 regions). Therefore **although national factors influence regional growth, regional factors in most cases largely determine the regions' international performance.** Among the regions that either increased or reduced their relative GDP share, in approximately half of them (in both cases) regional factors were responsible for no less than 25% of the overall change.

Components of growth associated with rural and urban regions

This report categorises regions into four groups based on average per capita GDP levels and growth rates. This typology is used to assess the key components contributing to growth in rural and urban regions.

- In urban regions productivity seems to be the main regional factor associated with growth, while labour market areas remain an area of opportunity. In urban regions gains in productivity are positively associated with GDP per capita growth rates. Participation rates declined in all categories of the typology and activity rates also declined in all categories, except in regions with lower GDP per capita and lower growth in GDP per capita. The effects of employment rates varied.
- In rural regions productivity also seems to be the main regional factor of growth and outmigration was a common threat to all rural regions. In contrast to urban regions the best performing rural regions increased their labour force. In rural regions productivity is also positively associated with GDP per capita growth rates. Population and activity rates declined in all four categories, while participation rates increased in all categories, except in regions with lower GDP per capita and lower growth in GDP per capita than the OECD average. Employment rates declined in all categories, except in regions with lower GDP per capita and lower growth in GDP per capita.

Which policies will help to promote regional growth?

Opportunities for growth exist in all regions and national governments should promote growth accordingly. Greater growth occurs when regions are able to mobilise their own local assets and resources, rather than depending on support from the national government. Regional policies can assist in this task and in this sense regional policies are not a zero sum game. Fostering growth, even in lagging regions, is in the interest of national governments as it contributes to national output without hindering growth opportunities elsewhere. Growth is often occurring even in lagging regions, while successful regions should also be nurtured.

This report's findings can provide policy makers with a better understanding of the key determinants of regional growth, the length of time needed for these factors to generate growth and the most successful combinations of factors. It argues that governments should:

- **Provide infrastructure as part of an integrated regional approach:** The analysis suggests that infrastructure alone has no impact on regional growth, unless regions are endowed with adequate levels of human capital and innovation. In other words, infrastructure is a necessary but insufficient condition for growth. The analysis also reveals that it requires on average approximately three years to positively influence growth.

- **Invest in human capital:** Regions with insufficient human capital will not grow, while those with increased levels will reap the benefits of endogenous elements of growth. The effects of investing in tertiary education on regional growth are also positive, after a period of approximately three years. Human capital also has a strong indirect impact on regional growth by increasing the rate of patenting. Thus, regional policies which promote infrastructural development will only be successful if human capital and innovation are also present.

- **Emphasise innovation and research and development:** Investments in R&D have a positive effect on patent activity in all categories considered, as do R&D expenditures by businesses, the public sector, higher education institutions and the private non-profit sector. However, innovation is a longer-term process and only appears to have a positive influence on regional growth after five years. Our results suggest that as capital and talent agglomerate they tend to positively influence growth in neighbouring regions. However, innovation remains a highly local element.

- **Focus on integrated regional policies:** Agglomeration economies are partly responsible for regional growth. Endogenous sources of growth such as human capital and innovation are more important than a region's physical distance from markets. Although a region with good accessibility to markets has an added advantage for its growth prospects, these also depend on the presence of human capital, innovation, infrastructure and economies of agglomeration. Proximity among the diverse local actors in a regional innovation system may well be a key ingredient. The performance of neighbouring regions is strongly correlated with a region's performance, suggesting that inter-regional trade and inter-regional linkages play an important role in regional growth.

ISBN 978-92-64-03945-2
How Regions Grow: Trends and Analysis
© OECD 2009

Chapter 1

Overall Growth Trends

Introduction

OECD regions vary more in their economic performance than do individual OECD countries (see Box 1.1 for a definition of regions). At the national level the main determinants of growth are macroeconomic factors, institutions and policies. The latter two factors have a strong regional dimension. OECD regions are very heterogeneous. Each is endowed with very different production capacities, comparative advantages, geographic characteristics, institutions, policies and assets. It is no surprise, therefore, that some regions are in a better position to reap the benefits of globalisation than others.

In this chapter we summarise general growth trends and variations among OECD regions in GDP, GDP per capita and GDP per worker. We compare these variations with national level variations; large differences imply inequality between well-performing and under-performing regions. We also analyse change in regional inequality over time – between 1995 and 2005 and between 1980 and 2005. We compare all OECD regions with each other (international comparison), as well as looking at changes over time for regions

---

Box 1.1. **The OECD's regional typology**

In any analytical study conducted at sub-national levels, defining the territorial unit is of prime importance, as the word *region* can mean very different things both within and among countries. In this publication, *region* is used to mean a sub-unit within a country, rather than supra-national groupings of countries.

How does the OECD classify regions within each member country? Its classification is based on two territorial levels. The higher level (Territorial Level 2 – TL2) consists of 335 large regions, while the lower level (Territorial Level 3 – TL3) is composed of 1 679 small regions. All the regions are defined within national borders and in most cases correspond to administrative regions. Each TL3 region is contained within a TL2 region.

This classification – which, for European countries, is largely consistent with the Eurostat classification – helps us compare regions at the same territorial level. Indeed these two levels, which are officially established and relatively stable in all member countries, are used as a framework for implementing regional policies in most countries.

For more information please see: OECD *Regions at a Glance, 2009.* OECD, Paris.

20

within individual OECD countries (intra-national comparison). Finally, we examine whether the gap between predominantly urban and rural regions has widened or narrowed over time.

Main findings

The main findings of Chapter 1 are as follows:

- **The economic performance of regions varies more than for countries.** GDP, GDP per capita and labour productivity vary more widely across OECD regions than across countries. The disparity in growth among OECD regions exceeded that among countries by almost three times between 1995 and 2005. These wide differences in economic performance highlight the great heterogeneity that exists in OECD regions as a result of differences in their comparative advantages, stages of development and public policies.

- **Predominantly rural, intermediate and predominantly urban regions vary significantly in their economic performance.** The majority of regions with above OECD average GDP per capita are urban regions, and the gap between urban and rural regions in terms of GDP per capita increased between 1995 and 2005. However, there is no single path to attaining sustainable growth rates: a significant number of urban regions grew faster than rural regions in terms of GDP per capita, but also a significant number of rural regions outperformed urban regions. Similarly, intermediate regions display performances both above and below the OECD average. This highlights that opportunities for growth exist in all types of regions.

- **Regional inequality increased between 1995 and 2005** in about 70% of OECD countries. Only eight OECD countries (Belgium, France, Germany, Italy, Japan, Mexico, Spain and Turkey) reduced disparities among TL2 regions and only seven (Austria, Germany, Italy, Japan, Mexico, Spain and Turkey) did so among TL3 regions (see Box 1.1 for definitions of TL2 and TL3 regions). **However, this result should be treated with caution.** A supplementary analysis (see background documents at *www.oecd.org/regional/min2009*) which covers a longer time period, from 1980-2005 for most OECD countries, reveals that although regional inequalities declined in approximately one-third of OECD countries (i.e. Spain, Portugal, Norway, Italy, Korea, Austria, France, Germany, the Netherlands, Belgium and Turkey), in ten of them they increased (i.e. Slovak Republic, Hungary, the Czech Republic, Greece, Ireland, Finland, the United States, the United Kingdom, Poland and Australia). There is no clear trend for the remaining OECD countries.

- **There is no conclusive evidence that the average GDP per capita of OECD regions began to converge during 1995-2005.** Two complementary analyses reveal no absolute convergence in GDP per capita among TL2 regions between 1995 and 2005. There was some convergence among TL3 regions.

- **Regional convergence during 1995-2005 is only conditional on factors associated with growth.** Convergence among TL2 regions occurs when the analysis accounts for key determinants of regional growth such as innovation, infrastructure and human capital.

- **Convergence is associated with the level of development (i.e. GDP per capita).** Richer regions from the bottom quartile of the GDP per capita distribution are growing faster than their counterparts, while poorer regions from the top three quartiles of GDP per capita distribution are growing fastest within their group. Thus, there is some convergence within this subgroup. The analysis in this report cannot differentiate the effects that regional polices (or their absence) have on convergence.

- **Regions with a larger GDP have steadier growth rates than regions with a smaller GDP.** When measured by their GDP share in the OECD, only small OECD TL2 regions display annual growth rates above 4% and below 1%. Medium and large regions rarely display negative annual average growth rates.

Trends in regional GDP, GDP per capita and productivity

Economic performance between 1995 and 2005 varied much more markedly across OECD regions than across countries. For example, the average annual GDP growth rate in real terms at the national level varied from 1.1% in Japan to 7.5% in Ireland between 1995 and 2005. Over the same period annual average growth rates in real GDP across TL2 regions (see Box 1.1) ranged from –1.7% in Berlin (Germany) to 8.5% in the southern and eastern regions of Ireland. The variation was even larger across TL3 regions, from a low annual average growth rate of –7.8% in Kilis (Turkey) to a high of 9.4% in south-west Ireland, almost three times larger than the variation across countries. OECD regions also displayed similar variations in GDP per capita and productivity levels (Table 1.1).

The spread of growth over the last ten years varied more among regions (within countries) than among countries. Turkey recorded the largest spread of growth among regions at both territorial levels (TL2 and TL3) for both GDP and GDP per capita (Table 1.2). At TL3, the diversity of GDP growth rates within Turkey (15.4 percentage points) exceeded the diversity in growth rates between all OECD countries (6.3 change in pp) by almost three times. France displayed the largest spread of growth (11 pp) in change in labour productivity among TL2 regions, almost twice as large as the spread in productivity between OECD countries (5.2 pp). Among TL3 regions the spread of growth in productivity levels was the largest in Germany (12.5 pp), more than double the national spread for all OECD countries (5.2 pp).

Table 1.1. **Spread of growth in GDP, GDP per capita and productivity across OECD countries, TL2 and TL3 regions, 1995-2005**

		Change in real GDP	Change in real GDP per capita	Change in GDP per worker (labour productivity)
Countries	Min.	1.1% (Japan)	1.0% (Japan)	−0.4% (Spain)
	Max.	7.7% (Ireland)	6.0% (Ireland)	4.8% Poland)
	Range	6.3 pp	5.0 pp	5.2 pp
TL2	Min.	−1.7% (Berlin, DEU)	−1.8% (Adana, TUR)	−3.8% (Champagne-Ardenne, FRA)
	Max.	8.5% (Southern and Eastern, IRL)	7.1% (Southern and Eastern, IRL)	7.1% (Podlaskie, POL)
	Range	10.2 pp	8.9 pp	10.9 pp
TL3	Min.	−7.8% (Kilis)	−6.2% (Kilis)	−5.4% (L'Aquila)
	Max.	9.4% (South-West, IRL)	8.7% (South-West, IRL)	11.1% (Südthüringen, DEU)
	Range	17.2 pp	14.9 pp	16.5 pp

* pp refers to percentage points.
Note: GDP data for Turkey are only available for 1995-2001, and for the United States for 1997-2005. TL3 data are not available for Australia, Canada, the United States and Mexico.
Source: OECD Stat and OECD Regional Database (2008).

Table 1.2. **Growth rate variations for GDP, GDP per capita and productivity within countries, TL2 and TL3 regions, 1995-2005**

		Real GDP	Real GDP per capita	Productivity
TL2	Min.	−0.9% (Balikesir)	−1.8% (Adana)	−3.8% (Champagne-Ardenne)
	Max.	4.5% (Zonguldak)	5.6% (Zonguldak)	6.2% (Corse)
	Range	5.4 pp (Turkey)	7.4 pp (Turkey)	10 pp (France)
TL3	Min.	−7.8% (Kilis)	−6.2% (Kilis)	−1.4% (Südheide)
	Max.	7.6% (Batman)	6.7% (Tunceli)	11.1% (Südthüringen)
	Range	15.4 pp (Turkey)	12.9 pp (Turkey)	12.5 pp (Germany)

Source: OECD Regional Database (2008).

These wide ranges in economic performance highlight the **great heterogeneity that exists in the performance of OECD regions**. They are the result of differences in their comparative advantages, stages of development and public policies.

This significant heterogeneity reveals that there is no single path to attaining sustainable growth rates. Comparing performances between types of OECD regions (i.e. predominately urban and rural regions) reveals that not only is there a significant number of urban regions growing faster than rural regions, but also a significant number of rural regions out-performing urban regions in terms of GDP per capita growth rates over the past decade (Figure 1.1). Similarly intermediate regions vary significantly (Figure 1.2). This means there are **opportunities for growth** in all OECD regions.

Figure 1.1. **Initial GDP per capita and annual average growth rates in GDP per capita among predominantly urban and rural OECD TL3 regions, 1995-2005**

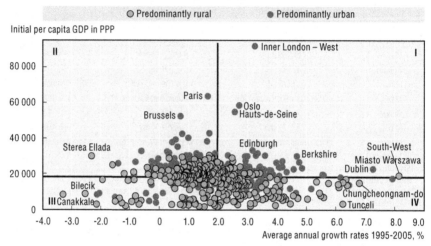

Source: Calculations based on OECD Regional Database (2008).

Figure 1.2. **Initial GDP per capita and annual average growth rates in GDP per capita among intermediate OECD TL3 regions, 1995-2005**

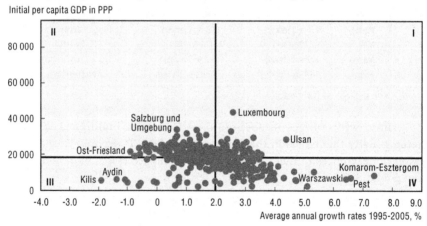

Source: Calculations based on OECD Regional Database (2008).

International comparison of regional growth rates: convergence or divergence?

An econometric analysis considering all regions allows us to explore two different (yet complementary) questions: i) Do lagging regions grow in general faster than richer ones, thus getting closer over time in terms of income per capita (this type of analysis is technically labelled *beta convergence*)? ii) Do disparities in GDP per capita among a group of regions diminish when comparing two points over time (technically known as *sigma convergence*)?

1. The analysis of beta convergence measures the relationship between the initial GDP of regions and their GDP per capita growth rates. A negative coefficient implies convergence, thus indicating that lower income regions on average grow faster and higher income regions on average grow more slowly. A positive coefficient implies divergence, indicating that richer regions grow even faster while poorer regions grow relatively more slowly.

2. The analysis of sigma convergence measures the change over time in the cross-sectional distribution (measured by the coefficient of variation) of GDP per capita (in logs). A decline in the coefficient of variation (less dispersion) over time implies convergence and an increase (more dispersion) implies divergence.

Beta convergence analysis yields very mixed results. While the larger unit of analysis (TL2) shows no sign of convergence at all, the finer level (TL3) of analysis evidences that convergence is taking place across OECD regions albeit at a very slow pace. Both beta and sigma analyses (Table 1.3 and Figure 1.3) find a mild rate of convergence in TL3 regions and no convergence in TL2 regions. However, further analysis is needed to investigate what factors are driving convergence and can explain growth. Although absolute convergence analysis (both sigma and beta) are most useful to establish trends, they are not intended to explain growth. Therefore, Chapter 3 will expand the analysis to conditional convergence and control for a series of factors and will include long-rung determinants of growth.

Despite no evidence of absolute convergence, Chapter 3 finds evidence of *conditional* convergence during the same period. This means that convergence

Table 1.3. **Beta convergence in TL2 and TL3 regions, 1995-2005**

Regions	TL2	TL2	TL3	TL3
GDP per capita 1995	−0.001	−0.001	−0.003	−0.004
	(−1.30)	(−1.42)	(−3.89)**	(−5.62)**
Annual national growth	–	0.707	–	0.644
		(12.15)**		(16.79)**
Constant	0.035	0.018	0.052	0.048
	(−3.17)**	(1.97)*	(6.08)**	(6.42)**
F-value	1.7	75.0	15.1	150.9
R^2	0.005	0.319	0.017	0.253
n	324	324	896	896

* Significant at 95%.
** Significant at 99%.
Source: Calculations based on *OECD Regional Database* (2008).

Figure 1.3. **Sigma convergence in TL2 and TL3 regions, 1995-2004**

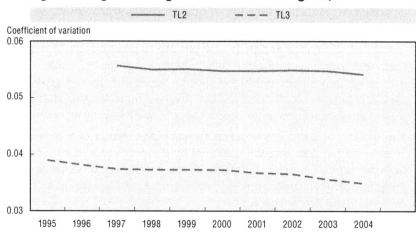

Note: The coefficient of variation is computed over the same set of regions where data are available. Therefore Turkish regions are not included in the sample as data are available only from 1995-2001, and the years 1995, 1996 for TL2 are excluded since TL2 GDP data are not available for the United States.

Source: Calculations based on *OECD Regional Database* (2008).

is indeed occurring when accounting for other factors influencing regional growth rates such as innovation, human capital and infrastructure. In addition the process of convergence can be associated with the level of development – in our case the level of GDP per capita – of countries and subsequently regions. Williamson (1965), applying Kuznets' famous inverted U-curve to analyse regional disparities, suggested that regional disparities decline once a certain level of development has been achieved.

We applied this hypothesis to OECD regions for the period 1995-2005 and found some, albeit limited, evidence of this trend. Regions in the bottom quartile of the GDP per capita distribution show a positive relationship between initial levels of GDP per capita and annual average growth rates, whereas the rest of the OECD regions – those belonging to the top three quartiles of GDP per capita – seems to be converging. In other words, the relatively richer regions from the bottom quartile of the GDP per capita distribution grow fastest within in this quartile, while the relatively poorer regions within the top three quartiles of GDP per capita distribution are the fastest growing regions, meaning that convergence is occurring within this sub-group. Visually (Figure 1.4), our TL2 sample of 335 regions seems to be in reality two samples – one sample in the bottom quartile of the GDP per capita distribution and the other made up of the remaining regions. Taken as a whole, a smooth inverted U-curve of the Kuznets type seems to appear. Our analysis cannot differentiate the effects that regional polices (or their absence) have on convergence.

Figure 1.4. **Scatterplot of average annual growth rates
for TL2 regions (1995-2005) and initial levels of income
(logged values of per capita GDP in 1995)**

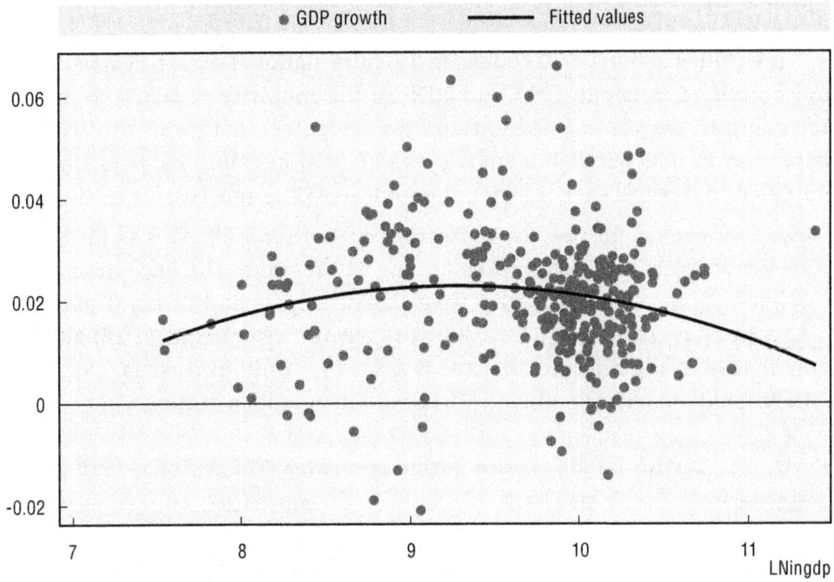

Source: Calculations based on OECD Regional Database (2008).

These results are confirmed in Table 1.4, where we apply a beta analysis to the two samples. The regression for the bottom quartile of regions (Model 1) – in terms of per capita GDP – shows a positive and statistically significant coefficient for initial level of income. That is, richer regions within that group of 82 regions are growing faster than lagging ones, a result that will lead to wider disparities over time within this subgroup. Conversely, a regression using the larger sample containing the top three quartiles (Model 2) shows that the rest of the OECD is converging. While the results for both processes of divergence and

Table 1.4. **Beta convergence in OECD regions: split sample
(TL2 regions, 1995-2005)**

	Model 1 bottom quartile "lagging regions"	Model 2 upper three quartiles "rest of OECD regions"
Initial GDP per capita	0.0099	−0.0062
	(2.48)**	(−2.67)**
F-value	6.13	7.15
R^2	0.059	0.028
n	83	249

* Significant at 95%.
** Significant at 99%.
Source: Calculations based on OECD Regional Database (2008).

convergence are statistically significant, the sizes of coefficients in both regressions – which show the speed of convergence – are rather small.

Intra-national comparison of regional growth rates

Inequities *within* OECD countries (*i.e.* intra-national disparities) persisted and amplified between 1995 and 2005 in the majority of OECD countries. According to the Gini coefficient and the weighted coefficient of variation, disparities in GDP per capita among regions (within countries) persisted and amplified in most OECD countries at both levels (TL2 and TL3):

- The Gini coefficient reveals an increase in territorial disparities in 70% (or 18 out of 26) of OECD countries among TL2 regions. The exceptions were Belgium, France, Germany, Italy Japan, Mexico, Spain and Turkey (Figure 1.5). At a finer regional grid (TL3), 73% of countries (or 19 out of 26) showed increases in regional imbalances (Figure 1.6). Only in Austria, Germany, Italy, Japan, Mexico, Spain and Turkey did inequalities decline.

Figure 1.5. **Territorial disparities within countries (TL2 regions, 1995-2005)**

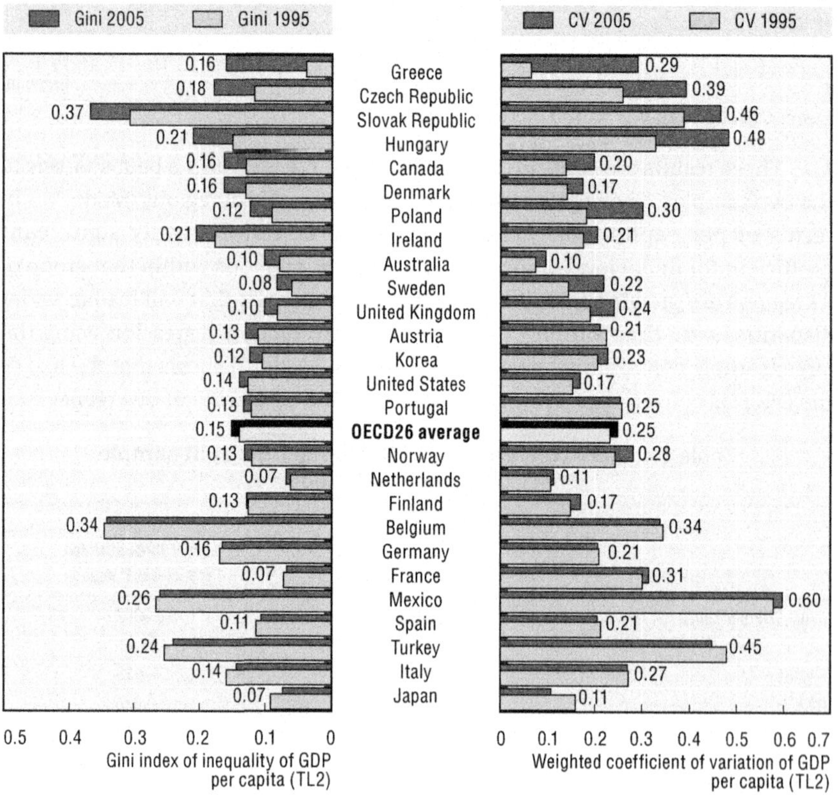

Source: Calculations based on OECD Regional Database (2008).

HOW REGIONS GROW: TRENDS AND ANALYSIS – ISBN 978-92-64-03945-2 – © OECD 2009

Figure 1.6. **Territorial disparities within countries (TL3 regions, 1995-2005)**

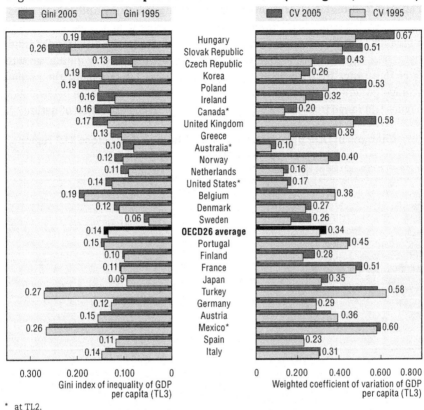

* at TL2.
Source: Calculations based on *OECD Regional Database* (2008).

- The weighted coefficient of variation was used as a complementary indicator to assess intra-national disparities and to look at their change over time. This indicator takes into account the overall size of regions by assigning more weight to larger regions (in terms of population) and less weight to smaller ones. For TL2 regions, the index revealed increasing regional imbalances in 70% of countries (exceptions being Belgium, Canada, Germany, Italy, Japan, Portugal, Spain and Turkey), and in 84% of countries for TL3 regions (except for Austria, Belgium, Spain and Turkey), see Figure 1.6.

A supplementary analysis (see background documents at *www.oecd.org/regional/min2009*) covering a longer time period, from 1980-2005 for most OECD countries,[1] reveals that regional inequalities declined in approximately one-third of OECD countries (*i.e.* Spain, Portugal, Norway, Italy, Korea, Austria, France, Germany, the Netherlands, Belgium and Turkey), while they increased in 10 of them (*i.e.* Slovak Republic, Hungary, the Czech Republic, Greece, Ireland, Finland, the United States, the United Kingdom, Poland and Australia). There is no clear trend for the remaining countries.

There is greater diversity in regional growth rates among smaller OECD TL2 and TL3 regional economies than among medium and larger ones. Regions with a larger GDP exhibit more uniform growth rates than regions with a smaller GDP. When measured by their GDP share in the OECD, only small OECD TL2 regions (with a total GDP share below 0.5%) display annual growth rates that range from above 4% to below 1% (Figure 1.7). Similarly, the annual average growth rates of TL3 regions with a total OECD GDP share below 0.25% (Figure 1.8) range from above 5% to below –1% (with the exception of Berlin).

Figure 1.7. **Changes in GDP per capita and initial share of GDP across TL2 regions, 1995-2005**

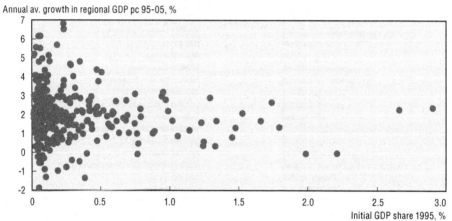

Note: The outlier regions Kanto and California are not included.
Source: Calculations based on OECD Regional Database (2008).

Figure 1.8. **Changes in GDP per capita and initial share of GDP across TL3 regions, 1995-2005**

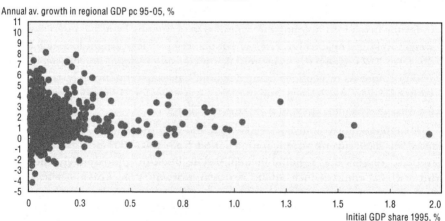

Note: The outlier regions Zonguldak, Bolu and Tokyo are not included.
Source: Calculations based on OECD Regional Database (2008).

The greater disparity in growth rates across smaller OECD regions could be explained by a number of factors: i) a statistical attribute (*i.e.* small numbers typically have more variability over time); ii) measurement errors (*i.e.* the measurement of GDP per capita in smaller regions may suffer from under and over-estimations when commuting trends amplify or change over time); iii) more vulnerability to external shocks (*i.e.* small regions are less diversified in their productive base and thus cannot trade-off changes across sectors to stabilise unexpected shocks); or iv) a catching-up process (*i.e.* the convergence process revealed in the beta analysis of TL3 regions). More work is needed to determine the influence of each of these factors on the greater diversity of growth rates among smaller regions.

OECD regions with middle to high GDP rarely display negative annual average growth rates. Out of the 19 TL2 regions with negative average growth rates, only two (Nordrhein-Westfalen and Niedersachsen in Germany) are meduim or large TL2 regions (*i.e.* with a share above 5% of the OECD GDP). Similarly, of the 66 TL3 regions with negative average growth rates, only 8 (Berlin, Köln, Bielefeld, Hannover and Bochum in Germany; Ketriki and Makedonia in Greece; Hyogo in Japan; Istanbul in Turkey) are considered medium or large regions (*i.e.* with an OECD GDP share larger than 0.25%).

A typology of regions

The relationship between GDP magnitude and growth across regions allows us to delineate a **typology of regions** in the OECD involving four categories:

- **QI:** regions with higher per capita GDP and growth than the OECD average (Quadrant I in Figures 1.9 and 1.10). These regions represent 23% and 20% of all TL2 and TL3 regions respectively. Ireland's Southern and Eastern (6.82%) regions, Bratislav Krajn (5.53%) in the Slovak Republic, and Northwest Territories and Nunavut (5.21%) in Canada recorded the highest annual growth rates in this category for the TL2 regions. Ireland's South-West (8.13%) and Dublin (7.24%) regions were the highest among the TL3 regions.

- **QII:** regions with higher per capita GDP but lower per capita GDP growth than the OECD average (Quadrant II in Figures 1.9 and 1.10). Regions in this quadrant represent the majority of TL2 and TL3 regions (33% and 35% respectively). Amongst the TL2 regions, Berlin (−1.35%) in Germany and Kentriki Ellada (−0.97%) in Greece recorded the lowest growth rates. Lowest amongst the TL3 regions were Sterea Ellada (−2.34%) in Greece and Südthüringen (−1.60%) in Germany.

- **QIII:** regions with both lower GDP and growth per capita than the OECD average (Quadrant III in Figures 1.9 and 1.10). This category represents the minority (18% and 17% respectively) of TL2 and TL3 regions. Of these,

Figure 1.9. **Level and growth of GDP per capita in TL2 OECD regions, 1995-2005**

Initial per capita GDP in PPP

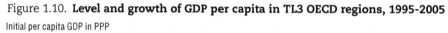

Source: Calculations based on OECD Regional Database (2008).

Figure 1.10. **Level and growth of GDP per capita in TL3 OECD regions, 1995-2005**

Initial per capita GDP in PPP

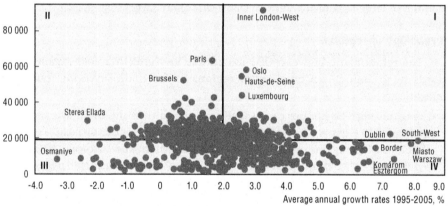

Note: The outlier regions Zonguldak and Bolu are not included.
Source: Calculations based on OECD Regional Database (2008).

Ankara (–2.07%) and Balkesir (–1.88%) in Turkey recorded the lowest growth rates for TL2 regions and Düzce (–13.79%), Osmaniye (–4.14%) and Çanakkale (–3.32%), also from Turkey, had the lowest growth rates in TL3.

- **QIV:** regions with lower GDP per capita but higher GDP per capita growth than the OECD average (Quadrant IV in Figures 1.9 and 1.10). These types of regions represent 27% and 28% of the TL2 and TL3 regions respectively. Mazowieckie (6.53%) in Poland and Ireland's Border, Midlands and Western regions (with a total growth rate of 6.17%) recorded the highest growth rates

HOW REGIONS GROW: TRENDS AND ANALYSIS – ISBN 978-92-64-03945-2 – © OECD 2009

of the TL2 regions; Miasto Warszawa (7.90%) in Poland and Komárom-Esztergom (7.36%) in Hungary were highest for TL3.

Most regions with above average levels of GDP per capita displayed lower than average growth rates in GDP per capita (Table 1.5). Among regions with below average GDP per capita there were more (27% for TL2 and 28% for TL3) displaying higher than average OECD growth rates. In contrast the majority of regions (32% for TL2 and 35% for TL3) with higher than average GDP per capita exhibited growth rates lower than the OECD average.

Table 1.5. **Average annual growth rate and income levels of regions by four categories, 1995-2005**

Percentage

	higher GDP/capita and higher growth in GDP/capita (QI)	higher GDP/capita and lower growth in GDP/capita (QII)	lower GDP/capita and lower growth in GDP/capita (QIII)	lower GDP/capita and higher growth in GDP/capita (QIV)
average annual growth rate (TL2)	2.89	1.12	0.99	3.20
share of regions (TL2)	23	32	18	27
average annual growth rate (TL3)	2.80	0.87	0.65	3.23
share of regions (TL3)	20	35	17	28

Source: Calculations based on OECD Regional Database (2008).

Urban and rural differences

Economic performance varies significantly according to whether the region is predominantly rural or urban. According to the OECD regional typology in 2005 (OECD Regions at a Glance, 2009), 27% of TL3 regions were classified as predominantly urban (PU), 38% as intermediate (IN) and 35% as predominantly rural (PR). The distribution of regions with GDP per capita above the OECD average reveals a larger share (34%) of urban regions. Likewise rural regions are more heavily represented in the group of regions with below average income per capita (Table 1.6).

Table 1.6. **Distribution of GDP growth per capita by regional type, TL3 2005**

Percentage

	PU	IN	PR	all regions
All TL3 regions	27	38	35	100
Regions with GDP per capita above the OECD average	34	39	27	100
Regions with GDP per capita below the OECD average	17	38	45	100

Note: PU = predominantly urban, IN = intermediate and PR = predominantly rural.
Source: Calculations based on OECD Regional Database (2008).

With regard to the four categories (Table 1.7), predominantly urban regions were the largest group (44%) among regions with higher per capita GDP and growth than the OECD average (QI). In contrast intermediate regions represented the largest group (38%) among regions with higher per capita GDP but lower per capita GDP growth than the OECD average (QII). They were the second largest group (38%) among regions with both lower GDP and growth per capita than the OECD average (QIII). Finally predominantly rural regions represented the largest group (47%) among regions with lower GDP per capita but higher GDP per capita growth than the OECD average (QIV).

Table 1.7. **Distribution of the four categories by regional type,
TL3 regions 1995-2005**

Percentage

	higher GDP/capita and higher growth in GDP/ capita (QI)	higher GDP/capita and lower growth in GDP/ capita (QII)	lower GDP/capita and lower growth in GDP/ capita (QIII)	lower GDP/capita and higher growth in GDP/ capita (QIV)
PU	44	28	19	16
IN	36	40	34	39
PR	20	31	47	44
all TL3 regions	100	100	100	100

Note: PU = predominantly urban, IN = intermediate and PR = predominantly rural.
Source: Calculations based on OECD *Regional Database* (2008).

Comparing the performances of predominantly urban and predominantly rural TL3 regions not only reveals a marked gap in per capita income but also, more worryingly, that this gap was widening between 1995 and 2005. In 1995, average per capita income in urban regions exceeded the OECD average by 21% (Table 1.8); in contrast average income in rural regions was just 85% of the OECD average. The gap between urban and rural regions increased over the decade 1995-2005, resulting in income in urban regions being 24% higher than the OECD average and rural regions being 84% of the average by 2005.

Table 1.8. **GDP per capita by regional type, TL3 regions 1995 and 2005**

Region type	1995		2005	
	Average GDPpc (PPP)	% of OECD av.	Average GDPpc (PPP)	% of OECD av.
PU	22 110	121%	27 111	124%
IN	18 169	99%	21 526	98%
PR	15 531	85%	18 533	84%

Note: PU = predominantly urban, IN = intermediate and PR = predominantly rural.
Source: Calculations based on OECD *Regional Database* (2008).

Despite the persistence of the overall gap, previous analysis displayed a significant number of rural regions outperforming urban regions, and likewise a significant number of urban regions performing better than rural ones. This means that opportunities for growth exist in all types of regions; whether regions achieve their growth potential will largely depend on their ability to mobilise their assets and resources. In the next chapter we make use of a benchmarking technique to tease out the common factors associated with successful and unsuccessful regions.

Note

1. Data for Greece, Ireland, Finland, The United Kingdom, Spain, Portugal, Italy, Austria, France, Netherlands and Belgium are available from 1980-2007; for the Slovak Republic, Hungary, Poland, The Czech Republic and Turkey from 1990-2007; for Australia from 1981-2007; for Norway from 1980-2005; for Korea from 1985-2005; for Germany from 1991-2007 and for the United States from 1963-2007.

ISBN 978-92-64-03945-2
How Regions Grow: Trends and Analysis
© OECD 2009

Chapter 2

Analysing the Components of GDP Growth

Introduction

In today's integrated world, regions are required to compete beyond national borders to remain competitive. There has been a recent paradigm shift in regional policies from subsidy dependency to integrated polices with growth-enhancing objectives. This has forced regions to compete in global markets to attract foreign direct investment, human capital and private firms from all over the world. Some regions have been successful in this task while others have not. This chapter examines common characteristics of successful and unsuccessful OECD regions. It does so by breaking regional growth rates down into: i) national factors; ii) labour productivity (GDP per worker); iii) population; iv) employment rates (employment to the labour force); v) participation rates (labour force compared to working age population); and vi) activity rates (working age population to total population). We then compare these components among successful and unsuccessful OECD regions.

This approach has allowed us to identify certain regions' components of success and to identify unused resources in others. We have also applied this accounting framework to predominantly urban, intermediate and predominantly rural regions to explore such questions as "What are the common growth component trends among the better and worse performing urban, intermediate and rural regions?"

Main findings

The components associated with fast-growing regions

- High national growth rates are associated with high regional growth rates. The direction of causation can run either way: just as national growth can influence regional performance, it might also be possible that high regional growth actually boosts national performance. As we will see below, national factors (country-specific conditions and characteristics that are common to all regions in a country, such as sound macro-economic policies) are a necessary but not sufficient condition for regional growth.

- Improvements in productivity (defined as average value-added per employed person) are also linked to high regional growth. This association is present when productivity gains occur alone, or simultaneously with gains in the employment to population ratio (i.e. the proportion of the population employed). Therefore there appears to be no trade-off between productivity and employment in fast growing regions.

- Labour markets are also important for fast-growing regions, especially when labour supply and labour demand increase simultaneously. More specifically, we found higher regional growth when the employment rate, the participation rate and the activity rate improved simultaneously.
- High population growth also appears to be common among the top 20 performing TL2 regions.

The components associated with slow-growing regions

- Localised factors (productivity, employment rates, participation rates, activity rates and population) seem to play a larger role than national factors in determining the poor performance of regions. For example, the 20 slowest growing TL2 and TL3 regions experienced a contraction in labour supply (activity rate) and loss of efficiency (productivity) rather than a decline in national factors.
- Among the localised factors, regional performance is particularly vulnerable to declines in the employment to population ratio, either when they occur alone or simultaneously with declines in labour productivity. Growth is slowest, however, when both factors decline simultaneously.
- When both labour supply (*i.e.* participation rates) and labour demand (*i.e.* employment rates) decline simultaneously growth can be significantly undermined.

The relative importance of national versus regional factors

Regional factors are not always correlated with national and common factors: a significant number of regions are: i) improving their overall position in the OECD despite a weak performance of their respective countries (20 regions); and ii) reducing their overall share despite gains in national factors (42 regions). Therefore **national factors, although necessary, are not sufficient in determining a region's successful international performance**.

Although national factors influence regional growth, regional factors in most cases largely determine the regions' international performance. Among the regions that either increased or reduced their relative GDP share, in approximately half of them (in both cases) regional factors were responsible for no less than 25% of the overall change.

Components of growth associated with rural and urban regions

We used our regional typology (Chapter 1), based on average per capita GDP levels and growth rates, to analyse components of growth in rural and urban regions:

- In urban regions productivity seems to be the main regional factor associated with growth, while labour market areas remain an area of opportunity. In urban regions gains in productivity are positively associated with GDP per capita growth rates. Participation rates declined in all categories of the typology and activity rates also declined in all categories, except in regions with lower GDP per capita and lower growth in GDP per capita. The effects of employment rates varied.

- In rural regions productivity also seems to be the main regional factor of growth and outmigration was a common threat to all rural regions. In contrast to urban regions the best performing rural regions increased their labour force. In rural regions productivity is also positively associated with GDP per capita growth rates. Population and activity rates declined in all four categories, while participation rates increased in all categories except in regions with lower GDP per capita and lower growth in GDP per capita than the OECD average. Employment rates declined in all categories except in regions with lower GDP per capita and lower growth in GDP per capita.

The approach: understanding the components of economic performance

Regional economic performance is the result of a combination of interconnected factors such as geography, demographics, specialisation, productivity, physical and human capital, infrastructure and the capacity to innovate, just to mention a few. Sometimes these factors reinforce each other; in other cases, they may counteract one another.

The analysis in this chapter breaks down growth (in the region's share of total OECD GDP) into six components following a similar approach as Spiezia and Weiler (2007):

- **Component 1. National and common factors:** national factors are country-specific conditions and characteristics that are common to all regions in a country. For instance, growth will tend to be higher in all regions of a country at the peak of its business cycle than in regions of a country in recession. Similarly, sound macroeconomic policies will benefit all of a country's regions and will result in relatively faster regional growth.

The remaining five components are **regional factors** (*i.e.* changes in the region's share of the country's GDP) (Figure 2.1):

- **Component 2. Population:** growth in regional population relative to national population growth.

- **Component 3. Labour productivity:** growth in regional labour productivity (GDP per worker) relative to national labour productivity growth. Productivity (average value added per employed person) is a proxy for the average level of productivity across all sectors and the degree of industry specialisation in that region.

Figure 2.1. **The components of regional growth rates**

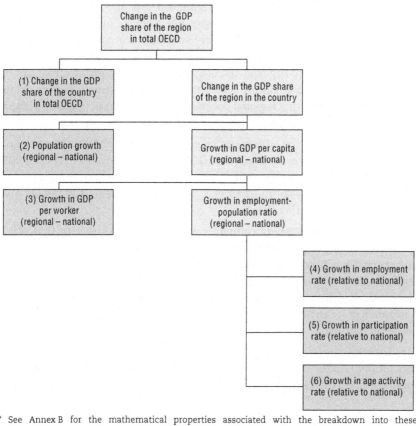

* See Annex B for the mathematical properties associated with the breakdown into these components.

- **Component 4. Employment rate:** growth in regional employment rate (employment to labour force ratio) relative to national employment rate growth. The employment rate reflects the efficiency of the local labour market.

- **Component 5. Participation rate:** growth in the regional participation rate (labour force to working age population ratio) relative to national participation rate growth. The participation rate summarises the characteristics of the regional working age population.

- **Component 6. Age activity rate:** growth in regional age activity rate (working age population to total population ratio) relative to national age activity rate growth. Age activity rates and population control for region-specific developments in age-structure and overall demographic growth.

There are some other region-specific factors to consider. Natural endowments in regions are region-specific features that tend to be constant over a prolonged period of time. The most obvious example is the presence of oil. Similarly, the rural or urban nature of a region will have an impact on its growth. Finally, performance also depends on regional policies, i.e. on the region's ability to increase productivity, change industry specialisation to seize new market opportunities, increase the efficiency of the local labour market, and invest in skills and in innovation. Regional assets are region-specific features that can be mobilised by appropriate policies. For instance, low-productivity regions would experience faster growth if regional policies were successful in upgrading labour skills and stimulating innovation (see Annex A for more details).

This categorisation allows us to calculate the contribution of each component to the overall change in GDP per capita in a variety of OECD regions. This list of components is by no means exhaustive; additional components are analysed in Chapter 3, which supplements the results and findings presented in this chapter.

Regional benchmarking compares a region's growth rate to that of all other OECD regions. Competitive regions grow faster than others by definition and therefore will raise their share of total GDP. In contrast less competitive regions will grow more slowly and their share of total OECD GDP will decline. The method of decomposition permits us to analyse growth in order to assess how much of it can be explained by each of the six components and to identify common patterns.

Each of these components can be viewed as an indicator of the determinants of economic performance at the regional level. Annex A gives more detail on the contribution of these factors to GDP growth.

Data analysis

Our analysis measured growth in the regions' GDP share for the six components described above. The period covered for OECD TL2 regions was 1995-2005 and 1999-2005 for TL3 regions. The time period has been reduced in TL2[1] regions when data for all six components were not available for the entire period. In this case the annual average growth rate covers a shorter period. In contrast when data are not available from 1999-2005 for TL3 regions they are not included in the sample. Data coverage totals 313[2] observations for TL2 regions and 815[3] for TL3 regions. Annex B provides a more detailed explanation of our analysis of these components.

Table 2.1 provides descriptive statistics for five components for TL2 and TL3 regions from 1995-2005.

Between 1995 and 2005 less than half of all OECD TL2 regions (112 regions out of 313) increased their share in total OECD GDP owing to regional and national factors. Over the same period a larger number of regions (201 out of 313) reduced their share in total OECD GDP.

Table 2.1. **Descriptive statistics of 5 components by TL2, TL3 and regional type**

	TL2 regions			TL3	
	1995	2005	Change	1999	2005
Population					
All regions	3 402 148	3 587 195	0.531%	633 296	649 060
PU				1 023 564	104 8472
IN				618 238	639 408
PR				332 852	334 993
Activity rates** (%)					
All regions	65.51%	66.51%	1.00%	66.1%	66.4%
PU				66.7%	67.6%
IN				66.5%	66.8%
PR				65.1%	65.5%
Participation rates**					
All regions	69.75%	70.13%	0.38%	69%	68%
PU				74%	71%
IN				68%	66%
PR				67%	68%
Employment rates** (%)					
All regions	64.49%	65.03%	0.54%	64%	62%
PU				69%	65%
IN				62%	61%
PR				61%	62%
Labour Productivity** (USD PPP)					
All regions	47 418	52 818	1.08%	50 355	53 920
PU				54 852	58 233
IN				50 370	53 903
PR				46 678	50 578

Note: PU = predominantly urban, IN = intermediate and PR = predominantly rural.
* pp refers to percentage points.
** *Definitions:* Activity rate is the ratio of working age to total population, participation rate is the ratio of the labour force to working age population, employment rate is the ratio of the labour force to working age population and productivity is the ratio of GDP to employed worker at place of work.
Source: OECD.Stat and *OECD Regional Database* (2008).

Figures 2.2 and 2.3 list the 20 best and worst performing TL2 and TL3 regions measured by the largest gains and losses in their GDP share in the OECD during 1995-2005 and 1999-2005 respectively.

Among the 20 fastest growing regions were:

● TL2 regions (Figure 2.2): **United States**: Nevada, Wyoming, Florida and Arizona; **Korea**: Chungcheong, Gyeonbuk, Gyeongnam, and the Capital Region, **Canada**: Alberta, Northwest Territories and Newfoundland and Labrador; **Ireland**: Border, Midlands Western and Southern and Eastern; **Australia**: Western Australia, Northern Territory and Queensland; **Hungary**:

Figure 2.2. **List of 20 fastest growing OECD TL2 regions, 1995-2005**

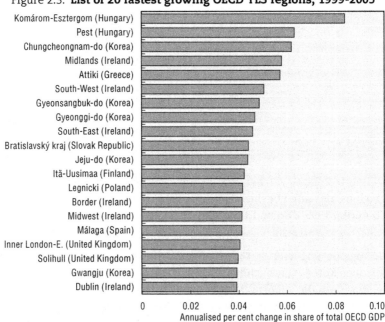

Alberta (Canada)
Chungcheong region (Korea)
Northern Territory (Australia)
Nevada (United States)
Newfoundland and Labrador (Canada)
Wyoming (United States)
Bratislav Kraj (Slovak Republic)
Quintana Roo (Mexico)
Border, Midlands and Western (Ireland)
Southern and Eastern (Ireland)
Gyeongbuk region (Korea)
Kosep-Magyarorszag (Hungary)
Western Australia (Australia)
Queensland (Australia)
Gyeongnam region (Korea)
Capital region (Korea)
Florida (United States)
Attiki (Greece)
Arizona (United States)
Murcia (Spain)

-1.0   0   1.0   2.0   3.0   4.0   5.0   6.0
Annualised per cent change in share of total OECD GDP

Source: Regions at a Glance 2009, OECD, Paris.

Figure 2.3. **List of 20 fastest growing OECD TL3 regions, 1999-2005**

Komárom-Esztergom (Hungary)
Pest (Hungary)
Chungcheongnam-do (Korea)
Midlands (Ireland)
Attiki (Greece)
South-West (Ireland)
Gyeonsangbuk-do (Korea)
Gyeonggi-do (Korea)
South-East (Ireland)
Bratislavský kraj (Slovak Republic)
Jeju-do (Korea)
Itä-Uusimaa (Finland)
Legnicki (Poland)
Border (Ireland)
Midwest (Ireland)
Málaga (Spain)
Inner London-E. (United Kingdom)
Solihull (United Kingdom)
Gwangju (Korea)
Dublin (Ireland)

0   0.02   0.04   0.06   0.08   0.10
Annualised per cent change in share of total OECD GDP

Source: Calculations based on OECD Regional Database (2008).

HOW REGIONS GROW: TRENDS AND ANALYSIS – ISBN 978-92-64-03945-2 – © OECD 2009

Kosep-Magyarorszag; **Mexico**: Quintana Roo; **Spain**: Murcia; and **Slovak Republic**: Bratislav Kraj.

- TL3 regions (Figure 2.3): **Korea**: Chungcheongnam-do, Gyeonsangbuk-do, Gyeonggi-do, Juju-do, Gwangju; **Ireland**: Midlands, South-West, South-East, Border, Midwest, Dublin; **Hungary**: Komárom-Esztergom, Pest; **United Kingdom**: Inner London-East, Solihull; **Greece**: Attiki; **Slovak Republic**: Bratislavský kraj; **Finland**: Itä-Uusimaa; **Poland**: Legnicki; **Spain**: Málaga.

Among the 20 slowest growing regions were:

- TL2 regions (Figure 2.4): **Italy**: Molise, Basilicata, Piemonte, Liguria, Valle D'Aosta, Bolzano-Bozen, Pulglia, Sicilia, Uumbria, Campania, Provincia Autonoma Di Trento; **Turkey**: Balikesir, Adana, Ankara, Bursa; **Germany**: Berlin; **Portugal**: Norte; **France**: Picardie; and **Greece**: Kentriki Ellada and Voreia Ellada.

Figure 2.4. **List of 20 slowest growing OECD TL2 regions, 1995-2005**

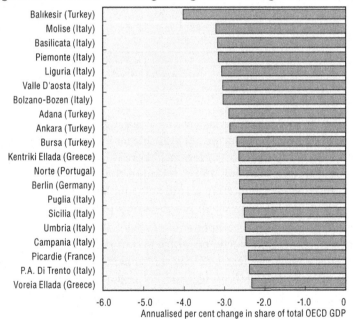

Source: Regions at a Glance 2009, OECD, Paris

- TL3 regions (Figure 2.5): **Greece:** Voreio Aigaio, Sterea Ellada, Dytiki Makedonia, Dytiki Ellada, Kentriki Makedonia, Anatoliki Makedonia and Thraki; **Italy**: Biella, Verbano-Cusio-Ossola, Imperia, Foggia, Brindisi, Agrigento, Siracusa, Oristano; **Germany:** Südheide, Göttingen, Lausitz-Spreewald, Berlin; **United Kingdom:** West Cumbria and **Austria:** Weinviertel.

Figure 2.5. **List of 20 slowest growing OECD TL3 regions, 1999-2005**

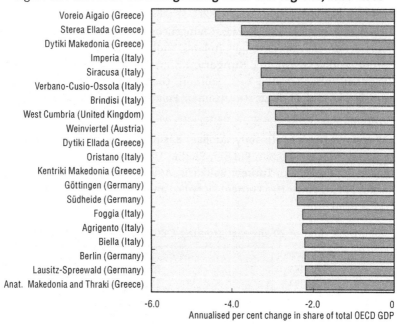

Source: Calculations based on *OECD Regional Database* (2008).

Whilst the ranking of the fastest and slowest growing regions should be interpreted with caution (data are not available for many TL3 regions and only from 1999-2005 for European TL2 regions), there is quite a number of regions from Korea, Ireland, Canada and the United States amongst the fastest growers. In contrast there are a significant number of regions from Italy, Turkey, Greece and Germany amongst the slowest performers.

By analysing the six components of regional growth combined with regional benchmarking, we have been able to compare the influence of the six components among the faster and slower growing regions, enabling us to detect which aspects lead to strong and weak regional performance.

Figures 2.6 to 2.8 display the overall movement in GDP share in the OECD in Europe and North America.

Figure 2.10 displays the contribution between 1995 and 2005 of the six components (expressed as gains and losses relative to the country's average growth) averaged over four regional groupings: *a)* the 20 fastest growing OECD TL2 regions; *b)* the 112 TL2 regions improving their GDP share in the OECD; *c)* the 20 slowest growing OECD TL2 regions; and *d)* the 201 TL2 regions decreasing their GDP share in the OECD.

Figure 2.6. **Change in the regional GDP share of the OECD: Europe**

TL2 regions, annual change 1999-2005

■ Higher than 2.0%
■ Between 1.0% and 2.0%
■ Between 0.0% and 1.0%
■ Between -1.0% and 0.0%
▨ Between -2.0% and -1.0%
▨ Lower than -2.0%
☐ Data not available

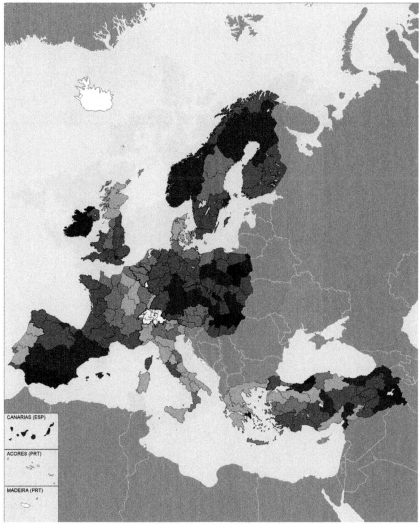

Graphs available at *www.oecd.org/gov/regional/statisticsindicators/explorer*.

Source: Calculations based on *OECD Regional Database* (2008).

Figure 2.7. **Change in the regional GDP share of the OECD: North America**

TL2 regions, annual change 1999-2005

■ Higher than 2.0%
■ Between 1.0% and 2.0%
■ Between 0.0% and 1.0%
■ Between -1.0% and 0.0%
■ Between -2.0% and -1.0%
▨ Lower than -2.0%
□ Data not available

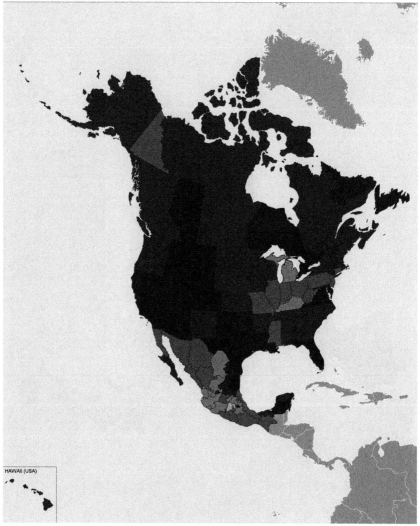

Graphs available at *www.oecd.org/gov/regional/statisticsindicators/explorer*.

Source: Calculations based on *OECD Regional Database* (2008).

Figure 2.8. **Change in the regional GDP share of the OECD due to change in population: Europe**

TL2 regions, annual change 1999-2005

■ Higher than 1.0%
■ Between 0.5% and 1.0%
■ Between 0.0% and 0.5%
■ Between -0.5% and 0.0%
▨ Between -1.0% and -0.5%
▨ Lower than -1.0%
□ Data not available

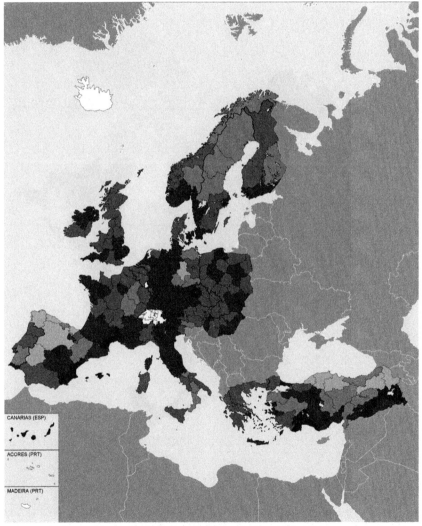

Graphs available at *www.oecd.org/gov/regional/statisticsindicators/explorer.*

Source: Calculations based on *OECD Regional Database* (2008).

Figure 2.9. **Change in the regional GDP share of the OECD due to change in the GDP share of the GDP per capita: North America**

TL2 regions, annual change 1999-2005

■ Higher than 1.0%
■ Between 0.5% and 1.0%
■ Between 0.0% and 0.5%
■ Between -0.5% and 0.0%
■ Between -1.0% and -0.5%
■ Lower than -1.0%
☐ Data not available

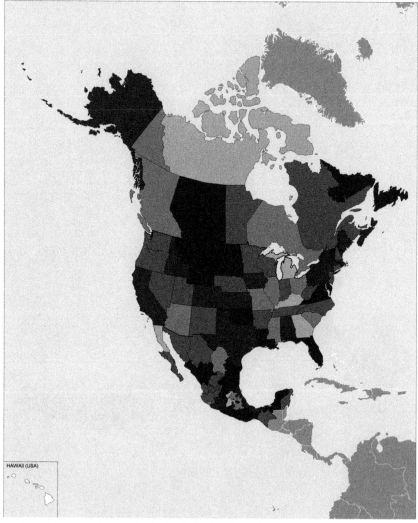

Graphs available at *www.oecd.org/gov/regional/statisticsindicators/explorer*.

Source: Calculations based on *OECD Regional Database* (2008).

Figure 2.10. **Contribution of each component averaged over the 20 fastest growing, 20 slowest growing, increasing and decreasing TL2 regions, 1995-2005**

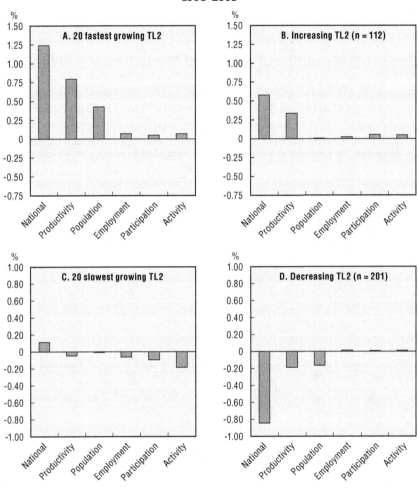

Source: Calculations based on *OECD Regional Database* (2008).

The trends for regional groupings (a) and (b) are similar: all six factors have contributed to growth in a positive way. The most important influence comes from national factors, followed by productivity. Nevertheless the contribution of population growth and the employment rate in the 20 fastest growing regions is much larger than among all the 112 successful regions. The former (*i.e.* population growth) might be due to migration.

The most important factors hindering growth among all declining regions (d) are national factors followed by productivity and finally population decline. In contrast, the most important factors hindering growth among the

20 slowest regions (c) are the activity rate (i.e. a reduction in the working-age population) and participation rate (i.e. labour supply), rather than national factors.

The results for TL3 are shown in Figure 2.11, which illustrates the influence of the six components (expressed as gains and losses relative to the country's average growth) averaged over four regional groupings: a) the 20 fastest growing OECD TL3 regions; b) the 458 successful TL3 regions (improving their GDP share in the OECD); c) the 20 slowest growing OECD TL3 regions; and d) the 357 TL3 regions decreasing their GDP share in the OECD.

Figure 2.11. **Contribution of each component averaged over the 20 fastest growing, 20 slowest growing, increasing and decreasing TL3 regions, 1999-2005**

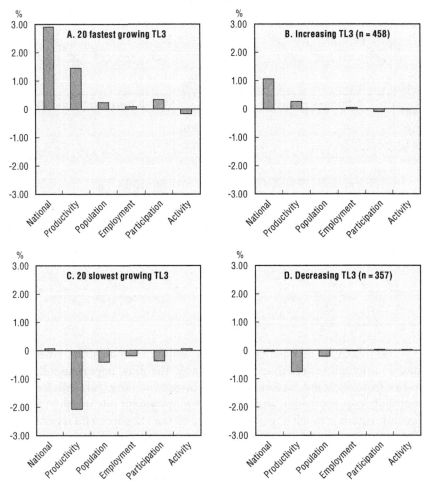

Source: Calculations based on OECD Regional Database (2008).

Again, in groupings (a) and (b) the most important influence on growth among TL3 regions comes from national factors, followed by productivity. Nevertheless in the 20 fastest-growing regions participation, population growth and employment also make positive contributions, unlike for grouping (b).

The effect of national factors on those regions decreasing their GDP share, both TL2 and TL3 (c and d in Figures 2.10 and 2.11) appears much less. Whilst in graphs (a) and (b) in Figures 2.10 and 2.11 national factors have a strong influence on the good performance of regions, localised factors (productivity, employment rates, participation rates, activity rates and population) rather than national factors seem to influence the poor performance of TL2 and TL3 regions with the exception of the 201 decreasing TL2 regions (graph d in Figure 2.10).

National and regional factors

Figure 2.12 compares national and regional effects among *fast growing* (i.e. top 20 performing regions and all regions increasing GDP share) and *slow growing* TL2 and TL3 regions (i.e. bottom 20 performing regions and all regions decreasing GDP share). It seems that national factors have a larger influence than regional factors among fast growing regions, although regional effects are quite large in the top 20 TL3 regions and in the 112 TL2 regions increasing their share. In contrast the effects are mixed in slow growing regions: **regional**

Figure 2.12. **National and regional influences on successful and unsuccessful TL2 and TL3 regions (1995-2005 for TL2 and 1999-2005 for TL3)**

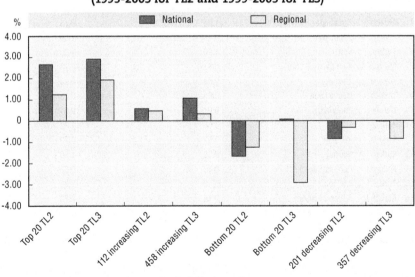

Source: Calculations based on *OECD Regional Database* (2008).

effects are mainly responsible for the poor performance of TL3 regions and national effects for the poor performance of TL2 regions.

Although national factors are relevant to the performance of regions, **regional factors in most cases also largely determine the regions' international performance**:

● In *more than half* of the 112 regions that increased their share in total OECD GDP (54%, or 60 regions), regional factors explain more than 25% of this increase. In 41% of them (62 out of 112) the increase due to region-specific factors was larger than the increase due to national and common factors.

● A similar importance of regional factors is observed among the 201 regions whose total share of OECD GDP is declining. In *more than half* of them (51% or 103 regions) regional factors were responsible for no less than 25% of the decline. In 30% (or 60) the decline due to region-specific factors was larger than the decline linked to national and common factors.

Regional factors are not always correlated with national and common factors. A significant number of regions are either improving their overall position in the OECD despite a weak performance of the country as a whole, or else have a declining overall share despite strong national gains. For example, Table 2.2

Table 2.2. **Regions improving their position despite weak national performance**

	Country	Regions	Changes in the GDP share of regions in OECD	Change in the GDP share of country in OECD
1	Mexico	Quintana Roo	2.80	−0.73
2	Greece	Attiki	2.01	−0.48
3	Mexico	Campeche	1.46	−0.73
4	Mexico	Tamaulipas	1.26	−0.73
5	Turkey	Zonguldak	1.18	−1.30
6	Turkey	Van	1.10	−1.30
7	Mexico	Baja California Sur	0.83	−0.73
8	Mexico	Tlaxcala	0.80	−0.73
9	Mexico	Nuevo Leon	0.65	−0.73
10	Germany	Thueringen	0.61	−0.61
11	Turkey	Hatay	0.60	−1.30
12	Mexico	Yucatan	0.57	−0.73
13	Turkey	Mardin	0.50	−1.30
14	Finland	Pohjois-Suomi	0.46	−0.32
15	Turkey	Trabzon	0.46	−1.30
16	Mexico	Aguascalientes	0.15	−0.73
17	Sweden	Oevre Norrland	0.14	−0.41
18	Germany	Bayern	0.12	−0.61
19	Turkey	Krkkale	0.04	−1.30
20	Sweden	Stockholm	0.01	−0.41

Source: Calculations based on *OECD Regional Database* (2008).

shows the 20 regions that were improving their overall relative position despite a weak performance of the country as a whole. The region of Quintana Roo, for instance, increased its GDP share in the OECD on average annually by 2.8%, although Mexico's share in the OECD declined (annually on average) by 0.73%. A similar pattern occurred in some other regions of Mexico, as well as in Turkey, Sweden, Germany, Greece and Finland.

Table 2.3 lists the 42 regions whose overall share in total GDP is declining despite improvements in the relative position of their countries. Among this group the region of Michigan experienced the largest decline in its total OECD GDP share (–1.77%) despite a relative improvement in the United States (0.57%). Many other regions in the United States, as in Poland and Spain, have had similar experiences.

Table 2.3. **Regions in decline despite strong national performance**

	Country	Regions	Changes in the GDP share of regions in OECD	Change in the GDP share of country in OECD
1	United States	Michigan	−1.77	0.57
2	Poland	Zachodniopomorskie	−1.37	0.01
3	United States	Kentucky	−1.12	0.57
4	Hungary	Nyugat-Dunantul/Western Transdanubia	−1.11	1.13
5	United States	Ohio	−0.93	0.57
6	Hungary	Del-Dunantul/Southern Transdanubia	−0.86	1.13
7	Poland	Lubelskie	−0.85	0.01
8	Poland	Swietokrzyskie	−0.80	0.01
9	Poland	Podkarpackie	−0.68	0.01
10	United States	Missouri	−0.67	0.57
11	United States	West Virginia	−0.59	0.57
12	Spain	Castilla-Leon	−0.55	0.30
13	United States	Illinois	−0.53	0.57
14	Poland	Opolskie	−0.53	0.01
15	Czech Republic	Severozapad	−0.52	0.44
16	Poland	Warminsko-Mazurskie	−0.52	0.01
17	United States	Mississippi	−0.51	0.57
18	Czech Republic	Severovychod	−0.48	0.44
19	Czech Republic	Stredni Morava	−0.46	0.44
20	Hungary	Del-Alfold/Southern Great Plain	−0.40	1.13
21	Poland	Dolnoslaskie	−0.39	0.01
22	Spain	Galicia	−0.32	0.30
23	Spain	Rioja	−0.29	0.30
24	United States	Connecticut	−0.26	0.57
25	United States	Indiana	−0.25	0.57
26	Poland	Pomorskie	−0.22	0.01
27	Slovak Republic	Stredne Slovensko	−0.22	0.91
28	Poland	Slaskie	−0.21	0.01

Table 2.3. **Regions in decline despite strong national performance** (cont.)

	Country	Regions	Changes in the GDP share of regions in OECD	Change in the GDP share of country in OECD
29	Poland	Kujawsko-Pomorskie	−0.19	0.01
30	Spain	Pais Vasco	−0.18	0.30
31	Canada	Yukon Territory	−0.18	1.33
32	United States	Pennsylvania	−0.16	0.57
33	Spain	Asturias	−0.16	0.30
34	United States	New Jersey	−0.12	0.57
35	Poland	Lubuskie	−0.05	0.01
36	United States	Nebraska	−0.05	0.57
37	Poland	Podlaskie	−0.04	0.01
38	Canada	New Brunswick	−0.03	1.33
39	United States	Wisconsin	−0.02	0.57
40	Spain	Aragon	−0.02	0.30
41	Poland	Lodzkie	−0.02	0.01
42	Spain	Navarra	−0.01	0.30

Source: Calculations based on OECD Regional Database (2008).

Components of growth in high performing regions

Of the 60 regions where regional factors had a large influence (i.e. above 25%) on the increase in their OECD GDP share, 13 of these regions' GDP share increase was due to a relative increase in population (Figure 2.13); in 24 there was a relative increase in GDP per capita and in the remaining 23 a relative increase in both components.

The highest relative population growth (i.e. growth difference in population between a region and its respective country) occurred in the Mexican region of Quintana Roo (3.55%) followed by Nevada (2.86%) in the United States, Baja California Norte (2.01%) in Mexico and Arizona (1.81%) in the United States. The regions with the highest GDP per capita growth were Zonguldak (5.24%) in Turkey, Newfoundland and Labrador (3.73%) in Canada and Wyoming (3.02%) in the United States.

Therefore, a significant number of regions (38% or 23 regions) were successful not only in increasing population but also in increasing GDP per capita.

On average, the increase in the regional GDP share – controlling for national effects – was largest for regions that managed to increase GDP per capita alone (1.46%), followed by regions that managed to increase both their population and their level of GDP per capita (1.30%). In contrast, regions that only increased their share in population growth (0.44%) recorded the lowest increase in GDP share.

Figure 2.13. **Analysing regional factors of high performing TL2 regions, 1995-2005**

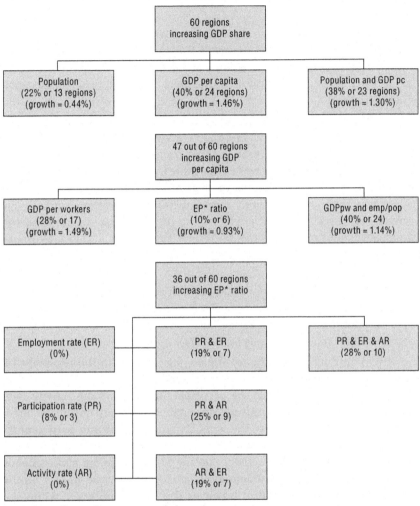

*   EP refers to the employment-to-population ratio.
All 60 regions have large regional factors (*i.e.* above 25%).

Among the 47 regions that increased their GDP per capita, the majority of them increased productivity either alone (28% or 17), or in combination with improved performance in their labour market (40% or 24). The remaining 10% (or 6) increased the employment-population ratio alone. Furthermore the rate of growth in total OECD GDP share due to productivity alone (1.49%) or in combination with the employment-population ratio (1.14%) was higher than the increase due to employment-population only (0.93%).

Therefore, improvements in productivity are an important factor for regional growth, either alone or with simultaneous improvements in labour markets.

The largest gains in productivity occurred in the Turkish regions Zonguldak (4.35), Van (3.68%), Hatay (3.17%), Mardin (3.11%), as well as in Thüringen (1.22%), Germany. The employment-population ratio grew most in Campeche (2.14%) in Mexico, Western Australia (1.4%) and the Spanish region of Cantabria (1.31%).

Of the 36 regions that increased the employment-population ratio relative to their country, almost one-third (28% or 10) increased all three rates (employment rate, the participation rates and the activity rate) simultaneously. The increase was entirely due to only one component in very few regions: 8% (or 3) of regions increased participation rates, and in no regions was the increase entirely due to the employment rate and the age activity rate. In 25% (or 9) of regions the increase was due to both the participation rate and activity rate, in 19% (or 7) it was due to the employment and activity rates, and in 19% (or 7) it was due to the employment and participation rates.

The employment rate grew the most in Andalucia (1.3%), Spain, and Oevre Norrland (0.6%), Sweden, while increases in the participation rate were largest in Campeche (2.0%) and San Luis Potosi (1.8%) in Mexico, Slaskie in Poland and the French Pays de la Loire (1.6%).

After controlling for national effects, the increase in the regional GDP share was on average larger for those regions that managed to increase all three rates (employment rate, the participation rates and the activity rate) simultaneously (1.45%). The impact of simultaneously improving in two out of the three labour components was similar: employment and participation increased regional GDP share by 1.05%, employment and activity rates by 1.03% and participation and activity rates by 1.02%. **Therefore simultaneous improvements in supply and demand factors have a strong impact on the employment population ratio; however the impact is larger when the relative size of the working age population also increases (i.e. activity rates)**.

Components of growth in low performing regions

Out of the 201 regions whose total OECD GDP share declined during 1995-2005, 103 of them were significantly influenced by regional factors (i.e. above 25%). In 19% (or 20) of these, the decline was due to a relative decrease in population (Figure 2.14), in 25% (or 26) it was due to a decline in GDP per capita, and in the remaining 55% (or 57) there was a decrease in both components. The lowest population growth occurred in Kastamonu (−2.7%) in Turkey and Asturias (−1.62%) and Castilla-Leon (−1.47%) in Spain, while the

Figure 2.14. **Analysing regional factors of low performing TL2 regions, 1995-2005**

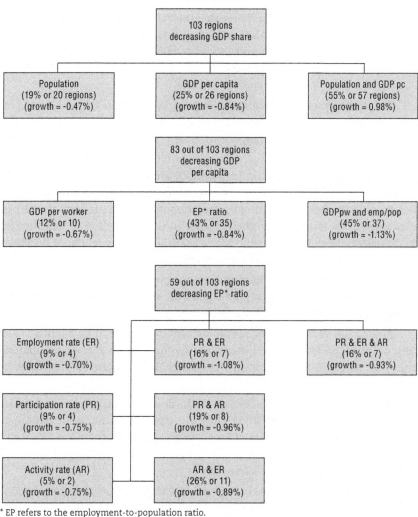

* EP refers to the employment-to-population ratio.
All 60 regions have large regional factors (i.e. above 25%).

lowest GDP per capita growth was in Nyugat-Dunantul/Western Transdanubia (–2.46%) in Hungary and Adana (–2.03%) in Turkey.

Therefore, a majority of slow-growing regions (55% or 57 regions) were unsuccessful in increasing **both population and GDP per inhabitant**.

On average the decrease in the regional GDP share – controlling for national effects – was largest for those regions whose population and level of GDP per capita both decreased (–0.98%). Nonetheless, the decrease in GDP share due to GDP per capita alone (–0.84%) was larger than the decrease due to population growth (–0.47%) alone.

Among the 83 regions that decreased their GDP per capita relative to their country's, most of them (45% or 39 regions) saw declines in both the employment-population ratio and GDP per worker simultaneously, while 43% (or 35) saw the employment-population ratio decline only and the remaining 12% (or 10) only saw GDP per worker declines.

The employment-population ratio grew the least in Berlin (–1.94%) in Germany and Zachodniopomorski (–1.19%) in Poland, while GDP per worker decreased the most in Champagne-Ardenne (–3.01%) in France and Ankara (–2.89%) in Turkey.

On average, the decrease in regional GDP share – controlling for national effects – was largest for those regions which experienced simultaneous declines in both their employment-population ratio and their level of GDP per worker (–1.13%). Nonetheless, the decrease in GDP share due to a decline in the employment-population ratio alone (–0.84%) was larger than a decrease due to a decline in growth in GDP per worker alone (–0.67%).

Therefore, declines in the employment-population rates are the most important factor hindering regional growth, either on their own or with simultaneous decreases in labour productivity.

Among the 59 regions whose employment-population ratio fell relative to their country's, in 19% (or 8) the decrease was entirely due to low participation rates and 9% (or 4) to low employment rates. None experienced declines in activity rates alone.

In the majority of regions (26% or 11) the decrease in the regional share in the OECD's GDP was due to both the rate of employment and participation, in 19% (or 8) it was due to the rate of employment and activity, and in 12% (or 5) it was due to the participation and activity rate. The remaining 16% (or 12) decreased all three rates simultaneously.

Furthermore the decrease in regional GDP share – controlling for national effects – was largest (–1.27%) when employment and participation rates decreased simultaneously. **Therefore, simultaneous declines in labour demand and supply factors are the most significant labour market factors hindering regional GDP growth.**

The employment rate grew the least in Navarra (–0.78%) in Spain, Provincia Autonoma di Bolzano-Bozen (–0.73%) in Italy and Berlin (–0.71%) in Germany. The participation rate grew the least in Podlaskie (–2.38) and Zachodniopomorskie (–1.56%) in Poland and in Kastamonu (–1.69%) in Turkey. The lowest growth in the age activity rate was recorded in Scotland (–0.54%) in the United Kingdom, Pais Vasco (–0.38%) in Spain and Liguria (–0.10%) in Italy.

Comparing the growth components in rural and urban regions

Based on past OECD territorial reviews[4] we generally expect the following common demographic and economic patterns in predominantly rural and predominantly urban OECD regions:

Rural regions:

- Population tends to decline in a significant number of rural regions such as in Mexico, Korea and the Eastern European countries, because of out-migration of young people – this may be especially the case in economically smaller rural TL3 regions, and in TL3 regions in general.

- Activity rates tend to diminish largely due to population aging in rural areas, and to a lesser extent to out-migration of the working age population (the elderly are more likely to stay behind).

- Participation rates tend to increase due to rising schooling levels that stimulate labour participation (especially women). This is especially true in low income OECD countries such as Mexico, Turkey and the Eastern European OECD countries.

- Employment rates may either increase or decrease. They will increase if out-migration creates greater employment opportunities for those staying or if rural economic diversification is dynamic enough. In small rural regions employment rates can rise substantially due to the small size of their labour force. However, the employment rate can decrease if economic diversification is not strong and, particularly, if the remaining workforce does not have suitable jobs (especially in economically weak regions).

- Productivity may increase or decrease. It will decrease if most of the out-migrants are highly productive skilled workers or when the skills of workers in rural areas do not match the available opportunities. Productivity may rise when out-migrants are low-productive labour-intensive workers or when rural regions enhance innovative activities or diversify their economies. Productivity may also be low when skills do not match the available opportunities in rural areas.

Urban regions:

- Population tends to increase because of in-migration from rural areas or outside the country.

- Activity rates tend to go up if younger immigrant workers and local young people reaching working age are more numerous than the elderly leaving the workforce.

- Participation rates are likely to increase due to advancement in schooling and because of rising costs of living in urban areas (brought about by lagging housing supply and congestion costs in public services). These factors induce households to increase their labour effort.

- Employment rates may either increase or decrease. They will decrease if the immigration rate is faster than jobs created from investment in urban areas (this would be especially the case in economically small regions); on the other hand, if work opportunities increase because of a dynamic economic expansion, city competitiveness and innovation, employment rates are likely to rise. Employment rates may also rise if nominal wages lag behind general price increases in cities due to wage negotiation or fast immigration.

- Productivity may go either way: up in dynamic urban areas that are succeeding in terms of diversification and innovation, or down in those failing on these grounds.

In this section we use the typology outlined in Chapter 1 (see Box 2.1) to analyse the influence of the six components among predominantly urban, intermediate and predominantly rural TL3 regions within each of the four quadrants in Figures 1.9 and 1.10.

Box 2.1. Typology of regions based on growth patterns

Q I: regions with **higher per capita GDP and growth** than the OECD average (Quadrant I in Figures 1.9 and 1.10).

Q II: regions with **higher per capita GDP but lower per capita GDP growth** than the OECD average (Quadrant II in Figures 1.9 and 1.10).

Q III: regions with both **lower GDP and growth per capita** than the OECD average (Quadrant III in Figures 1.9 and 1.10).

Q IV: regions with **lower GDP per capita but higher GDP per capita growth** than the OECD average (Quadrant IV in Figures 1.9 and 1.10).

See Chapter 1 for more details on this typology.

Figure 2.15 displays the average value of the six components in Quadrants I and IV, and Figure 2.16 shows them for Quadrants II and III, for TL3 regions in both cases. Among regions with higher GDP per capita growth than the OECD average, **national** effects (especially) and **productivity** are the most important factors influencing growth (Figure 2.15). Among regions with lower than average GDP per capita growth, **productivity** is the most important factor hindering growth (Figure 2.16), especially in urban regions from Quadrant III (*i.e.* regions with both lower than average GDP and GDP growth per capita). Among regions from Quadrant II (*i.e.* higher GDP per capita but

Figure 2.15. **Growth components and regional type, Quadrants I and IV, TL3 regions 1999-2005**

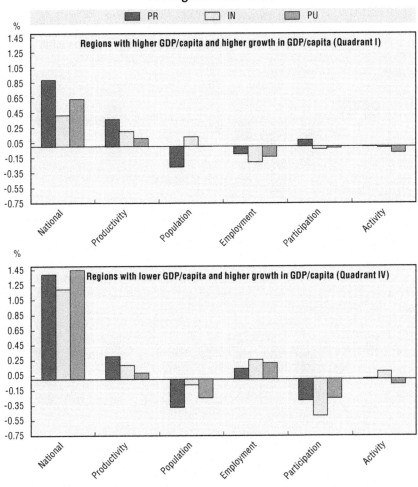

Note: PU = predominantly urban, IN = intermediate and PR = predominantly rural.
Source: Calculations based on *OECD Regional Database* (2008).

lower growth in GDP per capita) productivity declines were largest in intermediate regions. Therefore the weak performance in TL3 regions is mainly due to regional factors rather than national ones.

How does our analysis support the rural/urban hypothesis outlined above? In predominantly **rural regions**:

● Both population and activity rates declined in all four quadrants (as expected).

Figure 2.16. **Growth components and regional type, Quadrants II and III, TL3 regions 1999-2005**

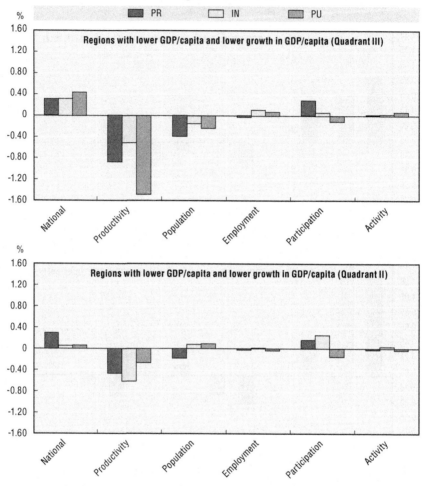

Note: PU = predominantly urban, IN = intermediate and PR = predominantly rural.
Source: Calculations based on *OECD Regional Database* (2008).

- Participation rates increased in all quadrants as expected and declined in regions with lower GDP per capita and lower growth in GDP per capita than the OECD average.

- Employment rates vary (as expected): they decreased in all quadrants except in Quadrant IV (i.e. regions with lower GDP per capita and lower growth in GDP per capita than the OECD average).

HOW REGIONS GROW: TRENDS AND ANALYSIS – ISBN 978-92-64-03945-2 – © OECD 2009

- Productivity as expected varied, increasing in regions with a positive GDP per capita growth rate (Quadrant I and IV) and decreasing in regions with a negative rate (Quadrants II and III).

In predominantly **urban regions**:

- Population increased in Quadrant I and II regions (as expected) but decreased in Quadrant III and IV regions (unexpected).

- Participation rates decreased in all quadrants (unexpected).

- Employment rates varied (as expected) – they increased in regions from Quadrants III and IV and decreased in regions from Quadrants I and II.

- Productivity, as expected, varied. It increased in regions with a positive GDP per capita growth rate (Quadrant I and IV) and decreased in regions with a negative rate (Quadrants II and III).

- Finally, activity rates only increased in regions from Quadrant III, while they decreased in the remaining three quadrants (unexpected).

The analysis in this chapter has broken down the components of regional growth, allowing us to associate common patterns among successful and unsuccessful regions. One important finding is that successful regions are associated with successful national growth rates, while unsuccessful regions are associated with poor performance in localised factors. In addition the analysis reveals that national factors are necessary, but not sufficient, to determine a region's successful international performance. Therefore there is a strong role for regional and localised factors. Among the regional components, high growth in labour productivity appears to be associated with high regional growth, while the effects of labour markets are most detrimental to regional GDP growth when both labour supply (*i.e.* participation rates) and labour demand (*i.e.* employment rates) indicators decline simultaneously.

However, one limitation of an analysis using growth accounting is that it cannot reveal the direction of causality, nor account for other relevant factors of growth, such as the role of innovation, economies of agglomeration, human capital, infrastructure, access to market and the effects of neighbouring regions. Thus the next chapter explores some of these determinants of growth using a number of econometric techniques.

Notes

1. In TL2 regions in Austria, Belgium, the Czech Republic, Denmark, Finland, France, Hungary, Ireland, Italy, the Netherlands, Poland, Portugal, the Slovak Republic, Spain, Sweden and the United Kingdom the time period ranges from 1999-2005, in TL2 regions in Mexico from 1998-2004, in TL3 regions in Norway from 1996-2005, in TL2 regions in Japan and the United States from 1997-2005, in TL2 regions in Turkey from 1995-2001, and in the rest of TL3 regions from 1995-2005.

2. Regional TL2 GDP data are not available for New Zealand, Switzerland and Iceland.

3. Regional TL3 GDP data are not available for Australia, Canada, United States, Mexico, New Zealand, Switzerland and Iceland.

4. OECD regional development work has involved a series of reviews at the national level. The countries already reviewed are: Italy, Korea, Hungary and Czech Republic, Japan, France, Luxembourg, Poland, Portugal, Norway, Finland and Chile, as Unitarian countries; Switzerland, Canada and Mexico as federal countries. Sweden's review is still being conducted. At the same time, the OECD has conducted thematic reviews that included regional case studies. Rural case studies were of Teruel (Spain), Tzumerka (Greece), Yucatan (Mexico), Sienna (Italy), and Morevska Trebova (Czech Republic); intermediate regions included Comarca Central Valenciana (Spain), Champagne-Ardenne (France), and Bergamo (Italy). Metropolitan regional reviews also included Athens, Busan, Helsinki, Øresund, Vienna/Bratislava, Melbourne, Montreal, Mexico City, Istanbul, Randstad, Milan, Madrid, Stockholm, Cape Town, Toronto, and Copenhagen. Ongoing metropolitan reviews are also being done of Venice and Guangdong.

ISBN 978-92-64-03945-2
How Regions Grow: Trends and Analysis
© OECD 2009

Chapter 3

Assessing the Impact of the Main Determinants of Regional Growth: A Parametric Analysis

Introduction

Chapter 1 described how, between 1995 and 2005, there was a significantly greater disparity in growth (three times larger) across OECD regions than across countries. Furthermore, we showed that growth does not occur uniformly within similar types of regions (i.e. predominately urban and rural regions). Not only was there a significant number of urban regions growing faster than rural regions, but also a significant number of rural regions out-performed urban regions in terms of GDP per capita growth rates over that decade.

The wide variation in economic performance among types of OECD regions reflects the regions' great heterogeneity in levels of income, rates of employment, mixes of high and low productivity activities, endogenous and exogenous assets, comparative advantages, stages of development and public policies. Therefore growth at the regional level results from a complex set of interconnected factors. Chapter 2 broke GDP growth down into a series of components (both endogenous and exogenous) so as to compare the performance of each region in terms of GDP growth associating common patterns in the decomposed components among successful and unsuccessful regions.

This chapter supplements that analysis. It investigates the impact of key structural endogenous factors on regional GDP growth while controlling for exogenous and national factors. The aim is to determine which factors are most relevant to generate growth at the regional level and which factors are needed if regions are to reap the benefits of globalisation. Are regions only required to improve their innovation capacity or do they also need to attract people, improve their infrastructure, and have an adequate labour market and business environment? Do regions need to improve only one of these factors or a bundle of them to remain competitive? We also distil the main drivers of growth and connect them with spatial aspects of agglomeration[1] to explore why some regions grow faster than others.

Main findings

We used four sets of analyses to explore trends and regional drivers of growth:

- A series of cross-section econometric models using elements stemming from neo-classical and endogenous growth theories along with the new economic geography (NEG, see Annex D).

- Dynamic econometric modelling through panel data analysis which allows for spatial analysis to interact with time.

- Analysis based on a knowledge production function that relates human capital and research and development (R&D) to innovation outcomes such as patenting activity.

- Spatial econometrics, to add a geographical element to the classical econometric methods.

These models show that regional dynamism depends on endogenous factors such as infrastructure, education, innovation, economies of agglomeration and geographic characteristics:

- *Human capital*: regions with insufficient human capital will not grow, while those with increased levels will reap the benefits of endogenous elements of growth. For example, regions with a low rate of tertiary education are less economically vibrant than those with a high rate. The long-term effects of tertiary education on regional growth are also positive. Human capital has a strong impact on regional growth both directly and indirectly by increasing the rate of patenting.

- *Innovation, research and development*: research and development (R&D) is an indirect determinant of growth through its impact on patenting activity. Investments in R&D have a positive effect on patent activity in all categories considered; expenditures by businesses, the public sector, higher education institutions and the private non-profit sector. However, innovation is a longer-term process. When measured as the number of patent applications, it only appears to have a positive influence on regional growth after five years. Our results suggest that as capital and talent agglomerate they tend to positively influence growth in neighbouring regions. However, innovation remains a highly local element that does not necessarily influence growth in neighbouring regions.

- *Distance from markets*: endogenous sources of growth such as human capital and innovation are more important than a region's physical distance from markets. Although a region with good accessibility to markets has an added advantage for its growth prospects, these also depend on the presence of human capital, innovation, infrastructure and economies of agglomeration. While distance from markets is not relevant for innovation, proximity among the diverse local actors in a regional innovation system may well remain a key ingredient for innovation.

- *Infrastructure*: infrastructure is a necessary, but not sufficient, condition for growth. It is only relevant if human capital and innovation are also present in a region. Infrastructure and human capital require three years to positively influence growth.

● *Spatial effects:* neighbouring regions and presence of agglomeration. Geographic space plays a role in determining innovation in these models as agglomeration economies emerge as a relevant determinant of growth rates. Our results go a step beyond what NEG theories would predict (see Annex D), by showing that agglomeration economies are partly responsible for regional growth. The performance of neighbouring regions is strongly correlated with the performance of any given region in the OECD, suggesting that inter-regional trade and inter-regional linkages play an important role in a region's performance.

The findings of the chapter are useful for policy applications and policy-makers by providing them with a better understanding of the impact of key determinants of regional growth, the length of time needed for these factors to generate growth and which combinations of factors are most successful.

These results suggest that in order to promote regional growth, policy-makers should develop a comprehensive regional policy that not only links regions through infrastructure investments, but that also fosters human capital formation and facilitates the process of innovation. The risk of piecemeal visions for regional policy, such as only promoting human capital or only providing infrastructure, is that a "leaking" (i.e. leaking of jobs, talent, etc.) instead of a linking process will be created.

Review of the literature: neo-classical, endogenous and new economic geography

Growth has been viewed by some as a process determined by the accumulation of physical and human capital (neo-classical theory); others see it also as a process linked to a place's characteristics, such as innovation, knowledge and human capital (endogenous growth). Neo-classical theories rely entirely on capital accumulation (Solow, 1956; Swan, 1956),[2] and although technology is considered to be important, modelling difficulties have meant that technology is considered to be exogenous (Barro, 1997) and therefore excluded from the models. More recently, however, technology has been brought into these models through the inclusion of R&D theories (Romer, 1990; Grossman and Helpman, 1994; Barro and Sala-i-Martin, 1995).

Together, these growth theories tell us that economic growth can be explained by the stock of physical capital, human capital and innovation. While these factors have been largely analysed at the national level, there is a strong regional and even local dimension to all three. Most notably, in the process of innovation, the interaction of economic agents and the exchange of ideas demand social capital, urban spaces and face-to-face interaction. This latter is necessary – despite the reduced telecommunication costs with the emergence of the Internet – for ideas, patents, R&D, or production-line improvements to become new or improved products or upgraded processes. In addition, the emergence of a new body of literature, the NEG (see Annex D) has given us fresh insights into the concentration and dispersion of economic activity. Thus, increasing returns to scale external to firms are the main incentive for workers and firms to agglomerate, but dispersion of economic activity is possible depending on the interaction of two sets of opposing forces under varying levels of transport costs.

Neo-classical and endogenous growth models

Neo-classical growth theory was originally based on the proposition that long-run growth is the result of continuous technological progress in the form of new goods, markets or processes (Aghion and Howitt, 1998). Otherwise, the lack of technological change in the long run would cease growth by the effects of diminishing returns (Solow, 1956; Swan, 1956). Thus, the model can be expressed as a function of capital accumulation only, assuming perfect competition and decreasing returns to capital leading to equilibrium (Ramsey, 1928; Solow, 1956). Technological progress is recognised as an important growth determinant, but is regarded as exogenous mainly due to the implicit difficulties in modelling increasing returns. What is more, the original model considers that people save a fraction of their income, whereas a proportion of it is lost through depreciation (Solow, 1956; Swan, 1956). Economic growth is, under these circumstances, temporary. In fact, "any attempt to boost growth by encouraging people to save more will ultimately fail" (Aghion and Howitt, 1998: 13). Even if population expansion is included, growth stagnation is the result. Population growth will reduce capital per person, not by destroying it as depreciation does, but by diluting it since the number of people that must use it has increased. Therefore, long-run per capita growth rates can only be explained by technological progress.

The way in which the original neo-classical model includes technological change is by considering that an exogenously determined constant rate reflects the progress made in technology (Solow, 1956; Swan, 1956). Thus, the model implies conditional convergence; that is, if a country starts from a lower level of per capita output relative to other economies, the former is expected to attain a higher growth rate. Hence, the countries' output levels will tend to converge. Indeed, economies with less capital per worker are likely to attain higher rates of return and growth (Barro, 1997). Such a convergence is based on the assumption of diminishing returns to capital.

The inclusion of human capital as another form of capital which determines growth was one of the improvements made to the original model. The first attempts to internalise technology faced the technical difficulty of modelling increasing returns to scale. One solution was to consider that technological progress is the result of learning by doing (Arrow, 1962). Another similar school of thought was that growth rates are related to investment rates and the underlying rate of new ideas (Kaldor, 1957). However, neither approach could avoid regarding part of the technological progress as exogenous. Thereafter, the models tried to use diminishing returns in the struggle to internalise technology (Aghion and Howitt, 1998).

In the absence of technological improvements, neo-classical approaches were incapable of explaining long-run growth (Barro, 1997). For endogenous growth theorists, long-run growth was contemplated by considering that returns to capital did not diminish, since human capital entailed knowledge spillovers and external benefits (Romer, 1986; Lucas, 1988; Rebelo, 1991).

There are two distinct views on the role of human capital in the endogenous growth models. One approach (Nelson and Phelps, 1966) views growth as primarily driven by the *stock* of human capital that in turn affects a country's ability to innovate to catch up with more advanced countries. Differences in growth rates across countries are then attributable to differences in human capital stocks and thus in those countries' abilities to generate new ideas and technical progress. This allows for a one-off increase in the stock of human capital to have an indefinite impact on growth. A different approach (Lucas, 1988 based on the contributions of Becker, 1964 and Uzawa, 1965) views the *accumulation* of human capital as the key determinant of growth. In this view, countries can only grow in the long run as long as human capital keeps accumulating over time.

In addition, R&D theories were introduced and imperfect competition was factored into the model (Romer, 1990; Grossman and Helpman, 1994; Barro and Sala-i-Martin, 1995). The pursuit of long-run growth determinants represents the major contribution of the endogenous growth approach (Pack, 1994).

However, there is common ground between the two theories (see Table in Annex C). The neo-classical approach regards growth as being determined by capital intensities and human capital, and recognises the role played by technology in determining long-run growth but fails to include it in the model. The endogenous growth theory agrees on all three elements, but instead of regarding technology as exogenous it has tried to include it in the analysis. Theoretically, technology-treatment differences are crucial for determining long-run growth; empirically however, it is difficult to test. Particularly, in cases where data are limited, including technological progress in the model is remarkably difficult.

Models of the new economic geography

Perhaps the biggest difference between the NEG and the neo-classical and endogenous approaches is the relevance of scale. Neo-classical and endogenous economic theory is only concerned with relative terms: consumers' choices, firms' decisions, and wage-setting are all determined at the margin. The outcome of this process is unaltered in an economy with one individual, 1 000 individuals or 1 000 000 individuals.

Scale effects, on the other hand, do matter in the NEG. The process of agglomeration is precisely concerned with scale effects, where small initial differences can cause large effects over time through a self-feeding mechanism.

The main idea behind the NEG is to explain why consumers and firms tend to agglomerate together in geographic areas where other firms and consumers are already located. Studies of this phenomenon include Perroux's notion of "growth poles" (1955), Myrdal's analysis of "circular and cumulative causation" (1957), and Hirshman's concept of "forward and backward linkages" (1958).

The NEG formalises these kinds of cumulative causation mechanisms. Krugman (1991) provided the theoretical foundations by showing how regions that are similar or even identical in underlying structure can endogenously differentiate into either rich "core" regions or poor "peripheral" regions through a self-feeding mechanism of circular causation. Since the publication of Krugman's 1991 paper, the literature has considerably evolved. NEG models have now been applied to a variety of topics (Table 3.1), and a more precise description of each model is given in Annex D.

Table 3.1. **Summary table: The new economic geography**

Model	Assumptions	Agglomeration forces	Prediction
Krugman (1991)	• Two regions • Agriculture and manufacturing (IRS) prod. • Labour mobility • Transportation costs	• Internal scale economies • Cost of transportation • Proportion of mobile population in response to wage differentials (demand linkage)	Low transportation costs and economies of scale will agglomerate production and labour migration in the region with a higher initial production.
Krugman and Venables (1995)	• Two regions • Agriculture and manufacturing prod (intermediate and final goods with IRS) • Transportation costs	• Internal scale economies • Cost of transportation • Forward (cost) linkage • Backward (demand) linkage	As transportation costs fall below a critical value the region with the larger manufacturing share attracts more firms due to forward and backward linkages increasing the real income of the core region relative to the periphery. If costs continue to fall wage differential induces firms to relocate back to peripheral regions (convergence).

Table 3.1. **Summary table: The new economic geography** (cont.)

Model	Assumptions	Agglomeration forces	Prediction
Venables (1996)	• Two locations (regions) • One sector producing competitive goods, and two monopolistic sectors vertically linked • Transportation costs	• Internal scale economies • Transportation cost • Forward (cost) linkage • Backward (demand) linkage	For high and low transportation costs firms locate in both locations (convergence). For intermediate transportation costs some firms agglomerate in a single location while others may spread out in response to factor price differences.
Krugman and Venables (1996)	• Two countries (regions) • Two industries prod. intermediate and final goods (IRS) • Transp. costs	• Internal scale economies • Cost of transportation • Forward (cost) and backward (demand) linkage	For high transportation costs each country maintains a full range of industries. Low transportation costs lead to agglomeration of each industry in the country with a stronger initial position. For intermediate costs agglomeration occurs only when industries are initially very unequally distributed.
Englmann and Walz (1995)	• Two countries • Same technology • Labour mobility for skilled immobility for non-skilled • Local goods and services, R&D goods, industrial goods	• Immobility of one factor of production • Nontradeability of local inputs • Local limitation of knowledge spillover (case 1)	Case 1 assumes spillovers occur only locally. Agglomeration always occurs in the region with an initial advantage in the number of intermediate goods yielding a core-periphery pattern. Case 2 allows for interregional spillovers – the solutions comprise a stable steady state equilibrium with equal growth rates in both regions.
Puga and Venables (1996,1997)	• N countries • Manufacturing IRS and agriculture CRS sector • Transportation/trade costs	• Internal scale economies • Trade/transportation cost • Immobility of labour • Forward (cost) linkage • Backward (demand) linkage	Industrialisation will only occur in a few countries. When forward and backward linkages are strong enough, agglomeration occurs in one country raising the level of wages until reaching a critical mass. Industries relocate to another country creating agglomeration. Thus industry will spill over in a series of waves from country to country.

Table 3.1. **Summary table: The new economic geography** (cont.)

Model	Assumptions	Agglomeration forces	Prediction
Puga (1998)	• Two regions each of them can provide a location for a city and an agricultural hinterland • Manufacturing IRS and agriculture CRS sector • Transportation costs • Mobility between regions and sectors	• Internal scale economies • Cost of spatial interaction causes firms and workers to locate close to good market access • Elasticity of labour supply	A balanced system of cities emerges under high transportation costs. When transportation costs are low and elasticity of labour supply is high, the model predicts a primate urban pattern. Thus the greater emergence of metropolises in the less developed countries and their scarcity in Europe are due to lower costs of spatial interaction, stronger economies of scale, and more elastic supply of labour to the urban centre.
Puga (1999)	• Two regions • Manufacturing IRS and agriculture CRS sector • Transportation costs • Mobility between sectors • Regional mobility (case 1) • No regional mobility (case 2)	• Internal scale economies • Trade/transportation cost • Forward (cost) linkage • Backward (demand) linkage • Elasticity of labour supply	Case 1: under regional mobility high trade costs yield convergence, and lower trade costs (beyond a threshold) yield agglomeration. Case 2: under no regional mobility there is convergence at high trade costs, agglomeration at intermediate costs, and convergence at low costs. Thus European integration brings agglomeration only if labour is mobile. If labour is not mobile there is agglomeration but this fades at lower costs.
Martin and Ottaviano (2001)	• Two countries (regions) • Immobility of labour • Composite (IRS) and homogenous (CRS) good • Innov. by patents	• Internal scale economies • Cost of transaction (cost linkage) • Immobility of labour (demand linkage)	If equilibrium is present initially there is no incentive to relocate production of the increasing returns sector. If there are more firms initially producing differentiated goods in one region, agglomeration occurs as the cost for innovation in that region will be lower. All innovation occurs in that region.

Note: IRS = increasing returns to scale; CRS = constant return to scale.

Generally speaking all NEG models share the following characteristics:

- Assumptions of imperfect competition through increasing returns to scale in an economic sector – the monopolistic Dixit-Stiglitz model (Krugman, 1991) is the preferred choice.
- Costs associated with trade or transportation.

- Forces enhancing (centripetal forces) or discouraging (centrifugal forces) agglomeration.

The first two items are embraced by all models, while the third item, centripetal and centrifugal forces, varies. The three proposed centripetal forces include:

- Migration of labour (labour mobility between regions).
- Forward and backward linkages.
- Elasticity of labour supply (labour mobility between sectors).

All three forces positively enhance the formation of clusters. Workers tend to migrate towards the region with a higher initial industrial production since more goods and services are produced there than in regions with lower industrial production. The arrival of people increases local demand and local profits which in turn attract even more firms offering more goods and services.

Producers of final goods will find greater industrial concentration more attractive because a larger base of intermediate producers gives rise to forward (cost) linkages, while producers of intermediate goods will find it advantageous to produce near the large final good industry giving rise to backward (demand) linkages. The elasticity of labour supply operates very similarly to labour migration between regions. A high elasticity attracts non-industrial workers from the same region, increasing local demand and local profits, further attracting more firms. Centrifugal forces develop through lower competition in peripheral regions. Lower competition raises profits, thus attracting more firms.

Agglomeration economies occur when a firm enjoys increasing returns to scale (IRS) in a particular place. This could either be because of the presence of natural advantages (i.e. natural resources, location, etc.), monopolistic protection, political reasons (e.g. the decision to create a capital city) or any other reason. The presence of IRS also induces other firms to locate there as people come in search of higher wages, job opportunities and cultural values.

There are three main mechanisms that work to produce agglomeration economies (Duranton and Puga, 2004):

1. Mechanisms that deal with sharing of:

   ❖ Indivisible facilities such as local public goods or facilities that serve several individuals or firms. Some examples, other than public goods, are facilities such as laboratories, universities and other large goods that cannot belong to one particular agent but where some exclusion is implicit in providing them.

   ❖ The gains from the wider variety of input suppliers that can be sustained by a larger final-goods industry. In other words, the presence of IRS along with forward and backward linkages allows firms to purchase intermediate inputs at lower costs.

❖ The gains from the narrower specialisation that can be sustained with higher production levels. Several firms specialise in producing complementary products, reducing overall production costs.

❖ Risks. This refers to Marshall's idea that an industry gains from having a constant market for skills; in Krugman's words, a pooled labour market. If there are market shocks, firms can adjust to changes in demand accordingly as they have access to a deep and broad labour market that allows them to expand or contract their demand for labour.

2. Matching mechanisms by which:

❖ Agglomeration improves the expected quality of matches between firms and workers, so both are better able to find a better match for their needs.

❖ An increase in the number of agents trying to match in the labour market also improves the probability of matching.

❖ Delays are alleviated. There is a possibility that contractual problems arising from renegotiation among buyers and suppliers result in one of the parties losing out by being held up by the other party in a renegotiation. This discourages investment. However, if the agglomeration is extensive enough, agents can change to an alternative partner.

3. Learning mechanisms based on:

❖ The generation, diffusion, and accumulation of knowledge. This refers not only to the learning of technologies, but also the acquisition of skills.

The main findings stemming from the basic formulation of the core-periphery model are summarised next:

● At high transport costs, there is only one possible outcome: production will be divided equally among the two locations (black centre dot Figure 3.1).

● If transport costs are reduced, for instance due to a new motorway, to an intermediate level, five possible equilibria are possible, three of which are also stable (black dots in Figure 3.1). At that level of transport costs, the equal division of production among the two regions continue to be possible (black centre dot Figure 3.1). However, any changes in labour force in either region triggers a process of partial concentration in favour of the region with the largest labour market while some production is still retained in the other region; these two possible equilibria are unstable (white dots Figure 3.1) and can eventually lead to a full – catastrophic – concentration in either of the two regions (northeast and southwest black dots Figure 3.1).

Figure 3.1. **Possible equilibria with intermediate transport costs (new economic geography)**

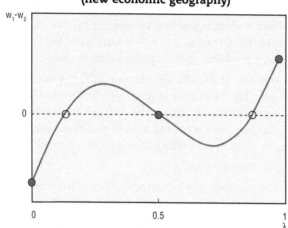

1. λ refers to the proportion of labour force, whereas w refers to wages.
2. Black dots refer to stable equilibria and white dots to unstable ones.
Source: Based on Fujita, Krugman and Venables (1999).

- If transport costs continue to fall to lower levels, firms find it easier to concentrate in either of the two regions and benefit from agglomeration economies, pooled labour markets and increasing returns to scale, and still ship part of the production to the other region.

In sum, NEG models explain why economic activity tends to concentrate in particular geographic spaces. They also reveal that the benefits of agglomeration economies are sometimes offset by the costs that arise with concentrations. It is no surprise, therefore, that the theory has not established a clear understanding – or framework – of the links between economic concentration and growth.

Growth at the regional level

Analytical framework and selection of variables

The analysis in this chapter uses a series of econometric models to investigate the impact of the main determinants of regional economic growth. The modelling techniques are i) cross-sectional ordinary least square (OLS); ii) panel data analysis; iii) analysis based on a knowledge production function; and iv) spatial econometrics.

We selected the main determinants of regional growth from the most relevant theories summarised above (the neoclassical and endogenous growth theory and the more recent NEG literature). The models do not only include traditional variables related to neo-classical growth theories, but also endogenous determinants. One of the most salient elements of neo-classical models is convergence, either absolute or conditional depending on the model taken into account. The implication of convergence is that poorer regions further away from their steady-state level will tend to grow faster and thus converge. One of the ways in which economic growth models try to test this hypothesis is by including initial levels of income. A negative sign in the estimated coefficient therefore would denote that lagging regions are catching up and convergence is taking place. Conversely, a positive sign would imply higher growth rates in already richer regions and thus divergence would be occurring.

In addition to the convergence hypothesis, neo-classical growth theories rely heavily on capital as the main determinant of economic growth. Lack of data at the regional level prevents us from using a measure of physical capital such as private investment or gross fixed capital formation. However, we use infrastructure in roads as a proxy for physical capital.

Endogenous growth theories stress the role of human capital and R&D as the sources of boundless growth opening up the possibility for non-convergence. In that sense, our model uses a measure of human capital stock. However lack of data at the regional level restricts our ability to capture the effects of quality in human capital.

Technological progress is accounted for in the model by using input and output innovation measures. The former refers to R&D expenditure, whereas the latter refers to patenting activity. Since the effects of innovation inputs might be indirectly related to regional growth, we explore the links between innovation inputs to innovation outputs through a knowledge production function. This function measures the impact on patenting of R&D expenditures, personnel and employment in knowledge-based sectors.

As explained earlier, the NEG discusses the centre-periphery model: increasing returns to scale, external economies and transportation costs. The mechanics of the model rely on the action of two countervailing forces: i) centripetal, inducing agglomeration; and ii) centrifugal, favouring dispersion. Agglomeration forces include: a pooled labour market, backward and forward linkages driven by the interaction of increasing returns and transportation costs, and technological spillovers. In contrast, centrifugal forces include factor immobility, land rents, congestion costs or pure diseconomies of scale. Thus, our model includes variables for labour market pooling, measures of agglomeration economies – captured thorough sectoral specialisation indices multiplied by their size – and geographical measures (both distance to markets and accessibility to markets) as proxies for transportations costs.

In order to measure the effects of these determinants of growth we selected the following indicators as structural variables in our models:

- Initial level of GDP per capita (convergence hypothesis/neo-classical):
  - ❖ Logarithm of initial GDP per capital expressed in 2000 USD purchasing power parity.
- A measure of physical capital (neo-classical):
  - ❖ Physical infrastructure – motorway density (total motorway kilometres in a region to its population).
- A measure of human capital (endogenous growth):
  - ❖ Stock of labour – attainment rates in primary and tertiary education (percent of the working age population with primary, secondary and tertiary education rates).
- A measure of intellectual capital (endogenous growth):
  - ❖ GDP expenditures on R&D by sector of performance (i.e. business, government, private non-profit, and higher education).
  - ❖ R&D personnel by sector of performance (i.e. business, government, private non-profit, and higher education).
  - ❖ Patent applications.
  - ❖ Employment in knowledge intensive sectors.
  - ❖ Employment in high and medium-high technology manufacturing.
- A measure of labour market performance:
  - ❖ Employment rates.
- A measure of agglomeration economies (NEG):
  - ❖ Specialisation in sector j multiplied by the size of sector j. The sectors of interest are financial intermediation, agriculture and manufacturing, and specialisation is measured using the specialisation index.[3]
- A geographical measure (NEG):
  - ❖ Distance from markets (by blocks, see Annex E).
  - ❖ Market accessibility (by blocks, see Annex E).

The impact of these structural variables on regional growth is estimated in the four econometric models. Coverage includes the period 1995-2005, and the main source of data is the OECD (2008) Regional Database (RDB) for most indicators, with the exceptions of infrastructure and geographic measures.

Cross-section model

Model specifications

The first econometric technique is a simple cross-section regression model in which regional GDP per capita growth during the period 1995-2005 is regressed on a number of key structural variables at the beginning of the period. The specification of the model is quite simple and it assumes a linear relationship as a starting point.

Based on the availability of data the static model takes the following functional form:

$$\frac{1}{T}\ln\left(\frac{GPD_{t+T}}{GDP_t}\right) = \alpha + \beta_1 \ln(Initial\ Y_t) + \beta_2 \ln(Infrast_t) + \beta_3 \ln(Prim\ Edu_t) + \beta_4 \ln(Tert\ Edu_t) +$$
$$+ \beta_5 (Empl\ Rate_t) + \beta_6 \ln(Patents_t) + \beta_7 \ln(R\&D\ Total_t) + \beta_8 \ln(R\&D\ BUS_t) + \beta_9 \ln(R\&D\ GOV_t)$$
$$+ \beta_{10} \ln(R\&D\ HE_t) + \beta_{11} \ln(Agg\ Ag_t) + \beta_{12} \ln(Agg\ Man_t) + \beta_{13} \ln(Agg\ Fin_t) + \beta_{14} \ln(Mkt\ Access_t)$$
$$+ \beta_{15} \ln(Dist\ Mkts_t) + u_t \qquad (1)$$

where t = 1995 and T = 10, and average growth of GDP is regressed on:

- $Initial\ Y_t$ = initial GDP per capita
- $Infrast_t$ = motorway density defined by kilometres of motorway to population
- $Prim\ Edu_t$ = primary educational attainments
- $Tert\ Edu_t$ = tertiary educational attainments
- $Empl\ Rate_t$ = initial year employment rates
- $Patents_t$ = patent applications
- $R\&D\ Total_t$ = total research and development expenditures
- $R\&D\ BUS_t$ = research and development expenditures carried out by firms
- $R\&D\ GOV_t$ = research and development expenditures carried out by the government
- $R\&D\ HE_t$ = research and development expenditures carried out by higher education institutions
- $AGG\ Ag_t$ = agglomeration economies in agriculture defined by the size of the sector (i.e. employment in agriculture) times the index of specialisation (see endnote 3) in agriculture
- $AGG\ Man_t$ = agglomeration economies in manufacturing defined by the size of the sector (i.e. employment in manufacturing) times the index of specialisation (see endnote 3) in manufacturing
- $AGG\ Fin_t$ = agglomeration economies in financial informediation defined by the size of the sector (i.e. employment in financial intermediation) times the index of specialisation (see endnote 3) in financial intermediation

- Mkt Access$_t$ = access to markets (see appendix E for full explanation)
- Dist Mkts$_t$ = distance to markets (see appendix E for full explanation)

The first explanatory variable (i.e. initial GDP per capita) is included to account for convergence or divergence of regional income. A negative sign in this variable would signal that relatively poorer regions are growing faster and therefore a process of convergence is under way. Conversely, a positive sign would indicate that richer regions are growing faster, and thus that regional incomes are diverging. This convergence or divergence trend will be conditional on a series of variables that determine growth, listed above. As economic growth theories argue that the forces behind long-run growth are physical capital, human capital and innovation, a number of variables have been introduced to model them. First, as capital stock data at the regional level are not available, a measure of infrastructure (motorways) was included. Second, human capital is included in the form of educational attainment for primary schooling and for tertiary education. Third, innovation enters into the model using patents and research and development (R&D) expenditures. Several variables that reflect expenditure in R&D were included, such as those carried out by the government, the private sector, higher education institutions, and non-profit organisations. In addition to economic-growth theory variables, a proxy for the proper functioning of labour markets was included in the form of employment rates.

The model attempts to explain regional growth not only by the usual determinants of growth, but also by using – as much as possible – variables that describe the dynamics of concentration and dispersion which can be argued to be at the heart of growth and inequality. One of the reasons for firms' agglomeration lies in backward and forward linkages and other agglomeration economies. The model incorporates these types of external economies into the firm by introducing sectoral specialisation indicators. Similarly, the NEG also argues that a second reason for agglomeration is thick markets. The model explores the impact of distance from or access to markets on economic growth.

Interpreting the results

The benefits of co-ordinating infrastructure, human capital formation and innovation

The results of the model during the period 1995-2005 imply that convergence is taking place across OECD TL2 regions, but that this is conditional on a series of factors (Table 3.2). Infrastructure does not affect regional growth by itself, except when education and innovation are considered (Models 6-7). Although infrastructure was included as a proxy for physical capital, relying on this measure presents two caveats. First, motorways are only one part of infrastructure (public capital) and other types of investment with direct impact on productive activities – either by enabling them or by reducing costs – such as energy, telecommunications, rail or airports, are not accounted for. Second, public investment in any case does not take into account private stocks of capital simply because data for that sector are not available at the regional level. Thus, not surprisingly the results are not significant on their own. Having said that, there might be a policy-related interpretation as infrastructure is only significant in the presence of human capital and innovation. Put simply, motorways may open up markets, but may also provoke fierce competition that may lead to either local firm mortality or migration of production to core regions. NEG models describe how goods may be shipped from the core to seize increasing returns to scale external to the firm. However, as human capital and innovation are present in the region, capital finds it attractive to stay in their regions and benefit from a pooled and well-matched labour market. Therefore, there is some suggestion that policies for infrastructure, human capital formation and innovation should be co-ordinated to boost economic growth in any region.

In terms of human capital, it is interesting to note that while primary schooling is negatively associated with growth, tertiary education positively affects regional performance. This is in line with what we would expect the model to show. Regions with insufficient human capital will not grow while those with increased levels will reap the benefits of endogenous elements of growth.

It is also important to note that employment rates do not significantly affect growth, although they do of course affect per capita income levels. One possible explanation is the position of the economy relative to its steady-state level. That is, the results for employment may reflect the mechanics of convergence. Regions with lower employment rates are not fully exploiting their labour resources and therefore are located far away from their ideal production possibilities. As with lower incomes, the reorganisation of the regional economy to seize unused labour potential results in higher growth rates.

Furthermore, innovation does positively affect growth just as endogenous growth theory suggests. However, this positive relationship between innovation and growth only holds for patenting, and not for total R&D expenditure. Although this initially may seem puzzling, it might be related to the very process of innovation. R&D expenditure is in fact one of the many inputs used in the process to produce innovation. Patenting is only one possible outcome and patents alone often fail to affect economic growth as many patents end up not being used by industry; they are often more an outcome of a broader process. In fact, if we think in terms of a knowledge production function, the result is not puzzling at all. R&D expenditures should be related to patenting, not directly to growth, so this indirect relationship with economic expansion may explain these results. This indirect relationship is supported by the results in Model 11, when R&D expenditure by source of funding is taken into account. The fact that business-based and higher-education-based expenditure on R&D are not significant – and even negative – is very revealing as these sectors are usually where the bulk of patenting takes place.

Agglomeration economies drive regional growth

A crucial result in our models relates to agglomeration economies. Just as NEG models suggest, agglomeration economies are an important element of concentration. Our results go a step beyond what NEG theories would predict, by showing that agglomeration economies are partly responsible for regional growth (Table 3.2). However, it is possible that there might be a strong correlation between tertiary education and innovation indicators as the significance of the variable drops in the presence of endogenous growth variables.

Table 3.2. **OLS cross section results for regional economic growth in OECD TL2 regions, 1995-2005**

	Model 1	Model 2	Model 3	Model 4	Model 5	Model 6	Model 7	Model 8	Model 9	Model 10	Model 11
Constant	0.0268	0.0013	0.1695	0.1553	0.1582	0.1934	0.193	0.3014	0.2972	0.104	-0.0126
	(2.65)**	(0.11)	(11.54)**	(9.06)**	(9.33)**	(6.44)**	(5.08)**	(6.27)**	(9.62)**	(1.46)	(-0.32)
Initial Y	-0.0006	0.0012	-0.0122	-0.0097	-0.0094	-0.015	-0.0152	-0.0261	-0.026	-0.0214	-0.0047
	(-0.59)	(0.95)	(-9.45)**	(-6.21)**	(-5.95)**	(-5.39)**	(-4.14)**	(-6.18)**	(-8.6)**	(-5.04)**	(-1.2)
Infrast	–	0.0075	–	0.0093	0.0132	0.0156	0.02	0.0155	0.0172	0.0148	0.0284
		(0.86)		(1.36)	(1.92)	(1.99)*	(2.31)*	(1.89)	(2.21)*	(1.89)	(3.23)**
Prim Edu	–	–	-0.0096	-0.0126	-0.0129	-0.0035	-0.004	-0.0075	-0.0079	-0.0091	–
			(-9.72)**	(-11.03)**	(-11.46)**	(-3.55)**	(-2.93)**	(-5.06)**	(-5.42)**	(-6.36)**	
Tert Edu	–	–	0.0076	0.0091	0.0097	–	–	0.0089	0.0087	0.0096	0.0067
			(8.79)**	(9.31)**	(9.81)**			(6.42)**	(6.83)**	(7.13)**	(4.58)**
Empl Rate	–	–	–	–	-0.0205	–	–	–	–	–	–
					(-2.37)**						
Patents	–	–	–	–	–	0.0015	–	–	–	–	–
						(2.5)**					
R&D Total	–	–	–	–	–	–	0.0019	-0.0007	–	-0.0009	–
							(1.71)	(-0.47)		(-0.6)	
R&D BUS	–	–	–	–	–	–	–	–	–	–	-0.0026
											(-2.3)*
R&D GOV	–	–	–	–	–	–	–	–	–	–	0.0028
											(2.98)**
R&D HE	–	–	–	–	–	–	–	–	–	–	-0.0078
											(-5.81)**
Agg Ag	–	–	–	–	–	–	–	-0.0014	-0.0009	-0.001	–
								(-2.04)*	(-1.41)	(-1.65)	

HOW REGIONS GROW: TRENDS AND ANALYSIS – ISBN 978-92-64-03945-2 – © OECD 2009

Table 3.2. **OLS cross section results for regional economic growth in OECD TL2 regions, 1995-2005** (cont.)

	Model 1	Model 2	Model 3	Model 4	Model 5	Model 6	Model 7	Model 8	Model 9	Model 10	Model 11
Agg Man	–	–	–	–	–	–	–	–0.0047	–0.0052	–0.0028	–
								(–2.89)**	(–3.62)**	(–1.77)	
Agg Fin	–	–	–	–	–	–	–	0.0029	0.0031	0.0014	0.0015
								(2.02)*	(2.32)*	(0.96)	(1.03)
Mkt Access	–	–	–	–	–	–	–	0.0002	0.0009	–	0.0013
								(0.39)	(1.75)		(2.19)*
Dist Mkts	–	–	–	–	–	–	–	–	–	0.0333	–
										(3.67)**	
R	0.0011	0.0082	0.2916	0.3235	0.3451	0.1652	0.1515	0.4712	0.4728	0.5111	0.4014
Adj R	–0.002	0.0019	0.2989	0.3134	0.3329	0.1505	0.1338	0.442	0.4493	0.4841	0.3717
F	0.35	1.29	40.93**	32.16**	28.24**	11.23**	8.57**	16.14**	20.17**	18.94**	13.5**
N	333	315	292	274	274	232	197	173	189	173	170

Note: */ Significant at the 95% confidence level; **/ Significant at the 99% confidence level; BUS = business sector; GOV = government sector; HE = higher education institutions
Countries missing as the model grows in variables due to lack of complete data mainly in R&D expenditure: Model 1: Iceland; Model 2: Australia, Norway and New Zealand; Model 3: Iceland, Denmark, Japan and Turkey; Models 4 and 5: Iceland, Denmark, Japan, Turkey, Australia, Norway and New Zealand; Model 6: Iceland, Denmark, Japan, Turkey, Australia, Norway, New Zealand and Switzerland; Model 7: Iceland, Denmark, Japan, Turkey, Australia, Norway, New Zealand, Switzerland, Belgium, Ireland, Sweden and Mexico; Model 8, 9 and 10: Iceland, Denmark, Japan, Turkey, Australia, Norway, New Zealand, Switzerland, Belgium, Ireland, Sweden, Mexico and Germany.
Source: Calculations based on OECD (2008) Regional Database.

Transport costs and markets: a complex relationship

Our most problematic results lie in the variables that try to reflect the NEG idea that transport costs and distance to relevant markets determine concentration. Our measure of distance to markets shows the opposite sign we would expect in Model 10, suggesting that being far away from markets has a *positive* influence on growth. Our interpretation is that the catch-up process evinced by the conditional convergence pattern shown in Models 3 to 10 implies that regions in the periphery are growing faster despite being relatively further away from the main markets at the core. In addition there might be a measurement bias given that our measures do not account for travel time and transportation networks and also that they are heavily affected by the size of TL2 regions.

A more promising result is obtained in our measure of accessibility to markets. Although this is statistically insignificant in Models 8 and 9, Model 11 suggests that a region with good accessibility has an added advantage to its growth prospects, though this depends on the presence of human capital, innovation, infrastructure and economies of agglomeration.

In any case, endogenous sources of growth such as human capital and innovation are more important than the physical distance to markets.

Similarly, agglomeration economies at play even in the periphery seem to be even more relevant than distance. In contrast, insignificant results for distance to markets and the fact that access to markets is only related to growth in the presence of human capital, innovation and infrastructure, seem to suggest that access to markets is a necessary but not sufficient condition for growth.

We should underline the fact that as more variables are included, the number of available observations falls, because data on all variables are not available for all countries. Finally, there is a strong change in the values and significance of coefficients of all explanatory variables when controls for country-effects are taken into account.

Panel data model

Model specifications

We used a panel data model to look at the effects of structural variables on regional growth over time. The structural variables and the time period are the same as in the cross-sectional model. A panel specification offers some advantages over the cross-sectional specification by permitting us to factor out the *time effects* and the *cross-sectional* components of the data. While the cross-sectional model measures the impact of initial values on regional growth over a longer time period (*i.e.* ten years), the panel model measures the yearly impact of the independent variables on growth, controlling for country effects (cross-section) and time effects. In addition, panel data approaches allow for lagged effects on the phenomenon to be explained, so if a particular variable, say infrastructure, takes time to have an impact because it needs to be built and used, these models allow us to pinpoint the time needed for that impact to emerge.

Other advantages of the panel specification are:

- It allows for a significant gain in data observations by using regional data in all years.

- It captures and controls for national and time effects on regional economic growth.

- It has the ability to measure the impact of independent variables over time. As already mentioned, this can be achieved by lagging the independent variables and measuring their effects over time.

In the panel specification the unit of analysis starts at the regional level. The *cross-sectional effects* then capture the effects of countries and the *time effects* capture the effects of time on regional growth. The model allows us to measure forces affecting regional growth at three distinct levels:

- Forces at the regional level are captured through the coefficients of the independent variables.

- The *cross-sectional effects* capture the variation common to all regions of a country after the regional effects are accounted for by the independent variable coefficients. These identify the national factors influencing regional growth.

- The *time effects* measure the variation common to all regions in a given year after the regional and country effects are controlled for.

The panel model is specified as:

$$\ln\left(\frac{GDP_{i,t}}{GDP_{i,t-1}}\right) = \alpha + \beta_1 \ln\left(Initial\ Y_{i,t-1}\right) + \beta_2 \ln\left(Infrast_{i,t-1}\right) + \beta_3 \ln\left(Prim\ Ed_{i,t-1}\right) + \beta_4 \ln\left(Tert\ Ed_{i,t-1}\right) +$$
$$+ \beta_5 \left(Emp\ Rate_{i,t-1}\right) - 1 + \beta_6 \ln\left(Patents_{i,t-1}\right) + \beta_7 \ln\left(R\&D\ Total_{i,t-1}\right) + \beta_8 \ln\left(R\&D\ BUS_{i,t-1}\right)$$
$$+ \beta_9 \ln\left(R\&D\ GOV_{i,t-1}\right) + \beta_{10} \ln\left(R\&D\ HE_{i,t-1}\right) + \beta_{11} \ln\left(Agg\ Ag_{i,t-1}\right) + \beta_{12} \ln\left(Agg\ Man_{i,t-1}\right)$$
$$+ \beta_{13} \ln\left(Agg\ Fin_{i,t-1}\right) + \beta_{14} \ln\left(Mkt\ Access_{i,t-1}\right) + \beta_{15} \ln\left(Dist\ Mkts_{i,t-1}\right) + u_i + e_{i,t} \qquad (2)$$

where the dependent and independent variables have already been specified in the previous section.

The panel model can be specified with fixed effects and random effects. One potential consequence of the fixed effect panel is that disturbances may be correlated within groups (*i.e.* countries). The random effects account for this correlation and therefore the random effects estimator should be selected, when possible, over the fixed effects estimator if it is statistically justifiable to do so since it offers more efficient estimates. A Hausman test can determine whether it is statistically justifiable to use random effects. For this reason Table 3.3 displays the results of the Hausman test for each model, whether it is statically justifiable, and whether it uses random effects (re) instead of fixed effects (fe).

Interpreting the results

- **Infrastructure:** As in the cross-section models, infrastructure does not influence regional growth by itself, but only in conjunction with human capital and innovation (Models 6-7), or with human capital, economics of agglomeration and accessibility (Models 8-9). Thus infrastructure is a necessary, but not sufficient, condition for growth.

- **Human capital:** The results for human capital variables confirm the findings of our cross-section models. Human capital influences growth: regional growth declines when there are insufficient levels of human capital (*i.e.* primary educational attainment rates) and it increases when

Table 3.3. **Panel results for regional economic growth in OECD TL2 regions, 1995-2005**

	Model 1	Model 2	Model 3	Model 4	Model 5	Model 6	Model 7	Model 8	Model 9	Model 10	Model 11
Constant	0.104	0.105	0.145	0.108	0.086	0.008	0.092	0.166	0.125	−0.082	0.052
	(4.99)**	(4.40)**	(5.55)**	(3.81)**	(2.95)**	(0.2)	(2.1)	(2.91)**	(2.70)**	(−0.88)	(0.9)
Initial Y	−0.008	−0.009	−0.008	−0.005	−0.001	0.002	−0.003	−0.010	−0.008	−0.009	0.0004
	(−3.97)**	(−3.7)**	(−3.37)**	(−1.82)*	(−0.18)	(0.6)	(−0.75)	(−1.98)*	(−1.76)*	(−1.75)*	(0.1)
Infrast	−	0.001	−	0.008	0.015	0.020	0.014	0.014	0.015	0.013	0.018
		(0.2)		(1.1)	(2.05)*	(2.50)*	(1.83)*	(1.6)	(1.84)*	(1.4)	(2.27)**
Prim Ed	−	−	−0.008	−0.008	−0.008	−0.002	−0.005	−0.009	−0.006	−0.008	−0.004
			(−5.15)**	(−4.94)**	(−5.00)**	(−1.32)	(−3.19)**	(−3.71)	(−2.58)**	(−3.42)**	(−2.31)**
Tert Ed	−	−	0.005	0.005	0.005	−	−	0.003	0.004	0.002	−
			(3.38)**	(2.97)**	(3.32)**			(1.1)	(1.5)	(0.8)	
Empl Rate	−	−	−	−	−0.049	−	−	−	−	−	−
					(−4.17)**						
Patents	−	−	−	−	−0.001	−	−	−	−	−	−
					(−0.86)						
R&D Total	−	−	−	−	−	−	0.001	−0.001	−	0.0002	−
							(0.8)	(−0.06)		(0.1)	
R&D BUS	−	−	−	−	−	−	−	−	−	−	−0.003
											(−2.96)**
R&D GOV	−	−	−	−	−	−	−	−	−	−	0.002
											(2.89)**
R&D HE	−	−	−	−	−	−	−	−	−	−	0.001
											(0.51)
Agg Ag	−	−	−	−	−	−	−	0.0003	0.001	0.0001	−
								(0.49)	(1.16)	(0.17)	
Agg Man	−	−	−	−	−	−	−	−0.002	−0.003	−0.001	−
								(−1.52)	(−2.28)*	(−0.80)	
Agg Fin	−	−	−	−	−	−	−	0.004	0.003	0.004	0.001
								(2.62)**	(2.31)*	(2.35)*	(0.72)
Mkt Access	−	−	−	−	−	−	−	−0.001	−0.0002	−	−0.001
								(−0.83)	(−0.35)		(−1.38)
Dist Mkts	−	−	−	−	−	−	−	−	−	0.052	−
										(3.32)**	
Fixed (fe) or Random (re)	re	re	re	re	re	fe	re	re	fe	re	fe
Hausman test (Prob>chi2)	0.26	0.15	0.80	0.37	0.35	0.00	0.19	0.10	0.04	0.54	0.00
R^2 within	0.005	0.006	0.017	0.022	0.035	0.022	0.027	0.037	0.030	0.047	0.070
R^2 between	0.016	0.001	0.334	0.372	0.326	0.000	0.296	0.505	0.456	0.359	0.041
R^2 overall	0.002	0.000	0.082	0.090	0.083	0.012	0.054	0.107	0.108	0.136	0.050
Wald chi (re), F (fe)	15.72	13.75	41.53	45.07	63.52	6.52	33.70	46.37	5.05	54.04	7.37
n	3 166	2 850	1 650	1 529	1 494	1 165	1 062	942	1 320	936	813

Note: */ Significant at the 95% confidence level; **/ Significant at the 99% confidence level; BUS = business sector; GOV = government sector; HE = higher education institutions.
Source: Calculations based on OECD Regional Database (2008).

sufficient flows of human capital (*i.e.* tertiary educational attainment rates) are present, although the effect in the latter case fades away in Models 8-10.

- **Employment:** Again the results for this variable support our cross-section models. Employment rates – when used as an indicator of a region's distance to its production possibility frontier – have an adverse effect on regional growth. This indicator captures a region's ability to mobilise labour resources: the further away the region is from the production possibility frontier the higher the region's growth potential.

- **Initial income:** These results are less stable and significant than in our cross-section models. The results of initial income (GDP per capita) on regional growth in the cross-section models are interpreted as convergence or divergence given the dynamics occur over the medium and long term. In the panel specification they show convergence (relative to the previous period) in Models 1-4 and 8-10 and no effect in the rest of models.

- **Innovation:** Patents have no effect on regional growth on a yearly basis, and expenditures in research and development only influence regional growth in Model 11 (positive effects for government expenditure and negative effects for business expenditure). Since patents do influence growth over a longer time period, a subsequent analysis measures the time period over which patents positively affect growth. Our interpretation of these results is that the effect of patents is relevant over the long-run, when patents can become new products, change or create new processes. Thus, there is a need to look more deeply into the inter-temporal relationship of patenting and growth (see below). In contrast, our results for R&D are quite similar to those of the cross-section models.

- **Agglomeration economies:** The results for this variable are consistent with those obtained through the cross-section analysis. External economies positively affect growth, mainly through financial intermediation. In contrast a lack of agglomerations – captured though specialisation in the agricultural sector multiplied by the size of the sector – does not hurt regional growth over a one year period.

- Finally **distance to markets** has a positive relationship with growth as in the cross-sectional model. Again this result might be due to a catching up-process taking place in regions distant from markets, such as those in the Eastern European countries. Or it might be due to limitations in our measure of distance to market, which is highly affected by the large size of several TL2 regions.

An important result obtained in the panel specification is that after controlling for national factors through the country dummies, regional factors are quite important in determining a region's growth path. This reveals that national factors are not sufficient at the regional level to mobilise the available assets.

The different effects of human capital (*i.e.* tertiary education), infrastructure and patents on regional growth obtained in the cross-section and panel specification models might reflect differences in the time dimension. It is often argued that some of these variables (human capital and innovation) are determinants of growth in the medium and long term. For these reasons the next section explores the effects of human capital, patents and infrastructure on regional growth over different time periods.

Effects of infrastructure, human capital and innovation on regional growth over time

Table 3.4 reports the effects of infrastructure, human capital and patents on regional growth over a three-year and a five-year period using four different models. The results for Models 3-4 (Table 3.4) should be interpreted with caution because they account for a relative small number of observations; however, Models 1-2 include sufficient observations. The results for all models show that all three variables appear to influence regional growth positively over the medium term. In the short term they do not influence growth, and in some cases they have an adverse effect on growth:

- **Infrastructure takes three years to contribute to growth** when innovation is present (Model 2), and five years when human capital is present (Model 1). In both models the effects of infrastructure reverse in the short run. A possible explanation is that it not only takes time for infrastructure to yield some benefits in terms of growth, but also that endogenous growth variables are present to avoid a leaking of economic activity instead of the desired link to markets.

- **Tertiary education only has a positive effect on growth after three years** (Models 3-4), while in the short run (Model 4) it has a negative effect. These results should be interpreted with caution given the small number of observations; however, the long-term effects of tertiary education on regional growth are positive and appear very robust in the cross-sectional specification.

- **Patent applications take five years to have a positive effect on regional growth** (Models 2-4), while over a shorter time frame they have a negative effect. Again the effects of patents on regional growth over the long term are positive (according to the cross-sectional models). As can be expected, the process of patenting – and of innovation more broadly – is long-term and influences growth only in the long run. However, the relationship between input and outcome variables in the process of innovation is not clear (such as the relationship between R&D or human capital and patenting). The next section attempts to shed some light on these associations.

Table 3.4. **Panel results, lagging human capital, infrastructure and patents in OECD TL2 regions, 1995-2005**

	Model 1	Model 2	Model 3	Model 4
Constant	-0.053	-0.043	0.324	0.258
	(-0.64)	(-1.52)	(-1.39)	(0.72)
Initial Y	0.013	0.004	-0.033	-0.045
	(-1.71)*	(1.60)	(-1.71)*	(-1.66)*
Infrast	0.023	-0.093	–	-0.233
	(0.22)	(-2.61)**		(-0.56)
Lag 3 Infrast	-0.239	0.175	–	-0.439
	(-2.00)*	(3.84)**		(-0.64)
Lag 5 Infrast	0.221	-0.047	–	0.760
	(3.57)**	(-1.19)		(1.46)
Primary Education	0.024	–	0.012	-0.088
	(1.52)		(0.30)	(-1.31)
Lag3 Primary Education	-0.008	–	0.023	0.098
	(-0.53)		(0.6)	(1.4)
Lag 5 Primary Education	-0.023	–	-0.062	-0.030
	(-1.34)		(-1.32)	(-0.045)
Tert Ed	-0.001	–	-0.031	-0.244
	(-0.07)		(-0.67)	(-2.74)**
Lag 3 Tert Ed	-0.009	–	0.108	0.319
	(-0.48)		(2.40)**	(2.74)**
Lag 5 Tert Ed	0.013	–	-0.046	-0.037
	(0.75)		(-1.20)	(-0.64)
Patents	–	-0.010	-0.010	-0.010
		(-5.83)**	(-1.00)	(-1.11)
Lag3 Patents	–	0.000	-0.019	-0.030
		(-0.14)	(-2.67)**	(-3.09)**
Lag5 Patents	–	0.006	0.022	0.032
		(3.83)*	(2.99)**	(-3.68)**
Fixed (fe) or Random (re)	fe	fe	re	re
Hausman test (Prob>chi2)	0.01	0.02	1.00	1.00
R^2 within	0.108	0.105	0.384	0.671
R^2 between	0.011	0.028	1.000	1.000
R^2 overall	0.022	0.020	0.501	0.749
Wald chi (re), F (fe)	3.08	15.63	29.15	53.63
n	283	958	40	32

Note: */ Significant at the 95% confidence level; **/ Significant at the 99% confidence level.
Source: Calculations based on OECD Regional Database (2008).

Knowledge production function

The analysis finds that patent applications, albeit an imperfect output measure of regional innovation, appear to have a positive influence on regional growth over a five-year (Table 3.4) and a ten-year period (Table 3.2).

This section estimates the coefficients of a knowledge production function at the regional level for determining the effects of input indicators on innovation. As the effects of innovation inputs on regional growth might be indirect, this section should shed some light on the mixed results obtained in the previous models on the impact of innovation inputs on regional growth (*i.e.* the cross-sectional model finds no impact of total R&D on regional growth, a negative effect in business and higher education R&D expenditures and a positive effect on government expenditures in R&D, Table 3.2).

Model specifications

Research on regional innovation generally falls into three main approaches (Box 3.1).

Box 3.1. **Three main models for regional innovation research**

The linear model

In this view, research leads to inventions which then become innovations and produce greater levels of productivity and ultimately output:

The empirical studies first determine a link between R&D and patents and then they estimate the link between patents and growth.

This view sees differences in innovation capacity arising from an endogenous growth perspective creating persistent differences in wealth and economic performance.

The higher the investment in R&D, the higher the innovative capacity and the higher the economic growth.

The linear model overlooks key factors about how innovation is actually generated.

Systems of innovation or learning region approaches

These approaches regard innovation as part of a territory-embedded process where institutional networks can favour (or deter) innovation generation:

The capacity of these networks to act as catalysts depends on the combination of social and structural conditions in every territory; these are often referred to as a *social filter*.

The proximity and interaction of local synergies are very relevant; importance is assigned to inter-organisational networks, financial and legal institutions, technical agencies and research infrastructures, education and training systems, governance structures and innovation policies.

> ## Box 3.1. **Three main models for regional innovation research** *(cont.)*
>
> These embedded networks in regions (*i.e.* social economic structures and institutions) are very difficult to measure and to compare.
>
> **Diffusion and assimilation of innovation:**
>
> The knowledge spillovers approach looks at the micro level in innovative units (*i.e.* R&D departments within firms, universities and research centres) as well as local institutions and individuals. The interaction – with each other and with their external environment through networks – produces the transmission of knowledge in the form of knowledge spillovers. However, this approach is also not easy to carry out as it is difficult to capture spillovers.
>
> *Source:* Crescenzi and Rodriguez Pose, 2006.

Our knowledge production function approach uses both the linear model and the systems of innovation approaches described in Box 3.1. We have not been able to capture knowledge spillovers, given the inherent difficulties of measuring them. Table 3.5 reports the coefficient of the knowledge production function, which measures the impact of the initial value of the independent variables on the final value of the dependent variable. The model is formally defined as:

$$\ln\left(Patents_{i,t+T}\right) = \alpha + \beta_1 \ln\left(Tert\ Ed_{i,t}\right) + \gamma_{j=1-4} \ln\left(R\&D\ Exp\ GDP_{j,i,t}\right) + \phi_{k=1-4} \ln\left(R\&D\ Personnel_{k,i,t}\right)$$
$$+ \beta_{10} \ln\left(KIS\ Emp_{i,t}\right) + \beta_{11} \ln\left(HTM\ Emp_{i,t}\right) + \beta_{12} \ln\left(Agg\ Ag_{i,t}\right) + \beta_{13} \ln\left(Agg\ Man_{i,t}\right)$$
$$+ \beta_{14} \ln\left(Agg\ Fin_{i,t}\right) + \beta_{15} \ln\left(Mkt\ Access_{i,t}\right) + \beta_{16} \ln\left(Dist\ Mkts_{i,t}\right) + e_{i,t} \qquad (3)$$

where t = 1995 and T = 10 R&D expenditures and R&D personnel include the (1) business and (2) government sectors, (3) higher education institutions and (4) the private non-profit sectors (*i.e.* j = 1-4 and k = 1-4 in Equation 3).

Interpreting the results

The results of the model are summarised below:

- Investments in R&D have a positive effect on patent activity in all categories considered; these are R&D expenditures by businesses, the public sector, higher education institutions and by the private non-profit sector. The fact that R&D expenditures in higher education institutions (HE) influences patenting activity negatively in Model 6 is quite puzzling and should be explored further. These results are also consistent with the previous models.

- R&D personnel only enhance patent applications in the business category, although the effects on patents are smaller than expenditures in R&D by the

Table 3.5. **Knowledge production function in OECD TL2 regions, 1995-2005**

	Model 1	Model 2	Model 3	Model 4	Model 5	Model 6	Model 7	Model 8	Model 9	Model 10	Model 11	Model 12	Model 13	Model 14	Model 15
Constant	-9.9	-9.4	-9.4	-10.2	-16.0	-14.3	-9.3	-13.6	-18.7	-16.9	-9.6	-7.5	-16.4	-5.0	-57.8
	(-11.68)**	(-8.73)**	(-8.70)**	(-8.88)**	(-9.56)**	(-8.64)**	(-5.04)**	(-7.08)**	(-8.12)**	(-6.93)**	(-10.06)**	(-6.49)**	(-6.17)**	(-0.55)	(-6.24)**
Tert Ed	1.2	1.1	1.1	1.2	1.6	1.5	1.0	1.6	2.3	1.6	1.1	0.8	1.2	1.1	1.1
	(16.30)**	(12.29)**	(12.12)**	(12.08)**	(11.39)**	(9.93)**	(6.41)**	(6.99)**	(7.09)**	(7.48)**	(12.86)**	(5.87)**	(16.20)**	(14.20)**	(3.77)**
R&D exp BUS to GDP	–	0.2	–	–	–	0.6	–	–	–	–	–	–	–	–	0.9
		(2.86)**				(1.96)*									(4.24)**
R&D exp GOV to GDP	–	–	0.9	–	–	0.8	–	–	–	–	–	–	–	–	–
			(2.22)**			(1.2)									
R&D exp HE to GDP	–	–	–	0.8	–	-2.4	–	–	–	–	–	–	–	–	–
				(1.69)*		(-2.87)**									
R&D exp in PNP to GDP	–	–	–	–	8.0	4.7	–	–	–	–	–	–	–	–	–
					(4.84)**	(5.48)**									
R&D personnel BUS	–	–	–	–	–	–	0.0001	–	–	–	–	–	–	–	0.00001
							(4.45)**								(1.0)
R&D personnel GOV	–	–	–	–	–	–	–	-0.2	–	–	–	–	–	–	-0.13
								(-1.2)							(-0.86)
R&D personnel HE	–	–	–	–	–	–	–	–	-0.7	–	–	–	–	–	–
									(-2.52)*						
R&D personnel PNP	–	–	–	–	–	–	–	–	–	0.2	–	–	–	–	–
										(1.5)					
KIS emp.	–	–	–	–	–	–	–	–	–	–	0.02	–	–	–	0.03
											(2.26)*				(1.17)
HTM emp.	–	–	–	–	–	–	–	–	–	–	0.1	–	–	–	0.02
											(1.66)*				(0.54)
Agg Ag	–	–	–	–	–	–	–	–	–	–	–	-0.2	–	–	0.03
												(-3.79)**			(0.32)

HOW REGIONS GROW: TRENDS AND ANALYSIS – ISBN 978-92-64-03945-2 – © OECD 2009

Table 3.5. **Knowledge production function in OECD TL2 regions, 1995-2005** (cont.)

	Model 1	Model 2	Model 3	Model 4	Model 5	Model 6	Model 7	Model 8	Model 9	Model 10	Model 11	Model 12	Model 13	Model 14	Model 15
Agg Man	–	–	–	–	–	–	–	–	–	–	–	0.1	–	–	0.02
												(0.6)			(0.09)
Agg Fin	–	–	–	–	–	–	–	–	–	–	–	0.4	–	–	0.06
												(2.72)**			(0.25)
Mkt Access	–	–	–	–	–	–	–	–	–	–	–	–	0.05	0.002	0.01
													(0.91)	(0.04)	(0.14)
Dist Mkts	–	–	–	–	–	–	–	–	–	–	–	–	1.4	-0.9	10.1
													(2.54)**	(-0.49)	(5.40)**
F-value	265.6	86.7	83.0	77.3	100.0	50.5	67.2	39.2	46.0	42.6	77.8	82.9	92.8	75.9	55.8
R^2	0.52	0.50	0.49	0.49	0.77	0.83	0.63	0.51	0.56	0.70	0.54	0.61	0.53	0.50	0.94
n	251	177	174	167	62	58	81	79	75	40	206	213	250	234	53

Note: */ Significant at the 95% confidence level; **/ Significant at the 99% confidence level; BUS = business sector; GOV = government sector; HE = higher education institutions; PNP = private non-profit sector; KIS = knowledge intensity services; HTM = high-and medium high-tech manufacturing.
Model 4 excludes 16 outlier regions, mostly from Australia, Canada and Turkey with a value of ln (distance to market) greater than 4.8.

Source: Calculations based on *OECD Regional Database* (2008).

business sector. The effects of personnel in higher education also appear negative; this is surprising but it might reflect the lack of R&D commercialization in higher education institutions. The small effects of R&D personnel on innovation reflect that fact that the marginal contribution of each person to innovation is not homogeneous across individuals; instead it varies significantly.

● As expected, the presence of knowledge intensive services and high technological manufacturing enhances regional innovation activity in terms of patent applications.

● The presence of economies of agglomeration only has a positive influence on innovation in the case of financial intermediation, while a lack of agglomeration economies reduces patenting activity.

● Finally, being distant from markets seems have a positive effect on innovation (Models 13 and 15), contrary to expectations, although this result is mostly driven by outlying regions.[4] When these regions are taken out of the sample (Model 14), the positive effect vanishes. This means that regional accessibility (and lack of it) does not influence patenting activities. These results suggest that a region's distance from markets or from other regions does not necessarily hinder its capacity to innovate, mainly because communication costs are falling. However, it is important to underline that while distance from markets is not relevant for innovation, proximity among the diverse local actors in a regional innovation system may well remain a key ingredient for innovation. However, our model does not include proximity among actors simply because it is difficult to measure.

In essence the evidence in this section supports the linear view (Box 3.1) in which human capital and R&D expenditure lead to innovation. It also shows that their influence is greater than R&D personnel. Within regional innovation systems, the presence of a specialised workforce – in high-tech manufacturing and knowledge intensive sectors – enhances innovation, as does the presence of economies of agglomeration.

Spatial econometric model

Model specifications

Spatial econometric techniques improve classical econometric methods when there is spatial dependence in the observations. Traditional econometrics have largely ignored these issues.[5] When spatial dependence is present in the data the coefficients estimated by classical econometric methods might be biased and inconsistent.

Spatial econometrics are generally characterised by: i) spatial dependence (or spatial autocorrelation) between sample data observations at various points in space (i.e. lack of independence which is often present among observations); and ii) spatial heterogeneity that arises from relationships or model parameters that vary with sample data as we move through space.

There are different types of spatial data, depending on whether the unit of analysis is an individual data point (e.g. geo-referenced or point pattern data, such as a firm or a household) or a geographical region (or areal data, such as administrative divisions). For each type of data, different techniques and models are used. For our area of interest (i.e. regions in OECD countries) we have areal (administrative) data.

Spatial dependence means that observations at location i depend on other observations at location $j \neq i$, i.e. $y_i = f(y_j)$, for $i = 1,...,n$ and $j \neq i$. We can allow the dependence to be among several observations by letting the index i take any value. To detect spatial patterns (association and autocorrelation), some standard global and local spatial statistics have been developed. These include Moran's I, Geary's C, G statistics, LISA and GLISA (see Annex F).

Two main reasons are commonly given for expecting to find dependence between data and spatial areas:

i) Data collection associated with spatial units might reflect measurement error. This would occur if the administrative boundaries do not accurately reflect the nature of the underlying process generating the sample data.

ii) The spatial dimension of socio-demographic, economic or regional activity may truly be an important aspect.

We therefore need to model the functional spatial dependence. Turning to spatial heterogeneity (the variation in the relationship over space), we might expect a different relationship to hold for every point in space. We cannot however hope to estimate a set of n parameter vectors given a sample of n observations: we simply do not have enough observations. We therefore need to provide a specification for the variation over space (i.e. we need to impose restrictions). Specifically, we need to formulate a parsimonious model which reflects the spatial structure in the data.

Because spatial relationships can be defined in an infinite number of ways, we impose a spatial structure on the data by constructing a *spatial weight matrix*, which portrays the neighbourhood structure among spatial units (see Annex F for more details). Spatial dependence is postulated to decrease with distance. We have two sources of information on distance: i) the location in Cartesian space represented by longitude and latitude (when we have geo-referenced data, where the distance between two points can be calculated); and ii) contiguity (for non-geo-referenced data), reflecting the relative position of one regional (spatial) unit to another such unit, e.g. two units are neighbours if they share a common border or edge, and for which we can sometimes calculate the centroid (geographical centre) coordinates and thus the distance between (the centre of) administrative units.

Therefore, the spatial structure (interconnectedness) of administrative units such as TL2 OECD regions can be represented by a weight matrix based either on contiguity criteria and/or on the geographical distance between centroids (or other spatial units such as main cities).

Once we have specified a spatial structure, we can use the spatial weight matrix in a spatial model, which will provide unbiased and consistent estimates in presence of spatial dependence (see Annex F for a brief description of the main spatial models).

Interpreting the results

Figures 3.2-3.4 plot the value of GDP PPP per capita (for 1995 and 2004), and GDP PPP per capita growth (1995-2005 period) for all OECD TL2 regions as well as their respective value in neighbouring regions (their spatial lags). The

Figure 3.2. **Moran scatterplot of TL2 regions GDP per capita in PPP, 1995**

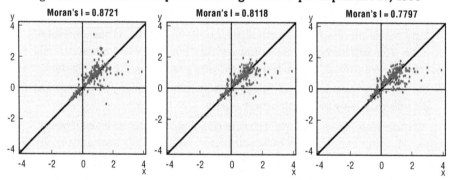

Source: Calculations based on OECD Regional Database (2008).

Figure 3.3. **Moran scatterplot of TL2 regions GDP per capita in PPP, 2004**

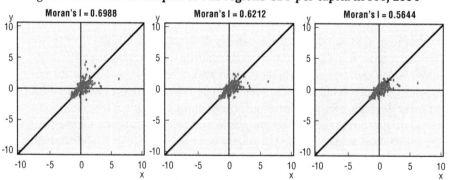

Source: Calculations based on OECD Regional Database (2008).

Figure 3.4. **Moran scatterplot of TL2 regions growth in GDP per capita PPP, 1995-2005**

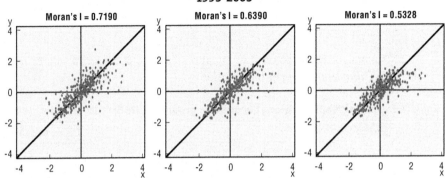

Source: Calculations based on *OECD Regional Database* (2008).

graphs are divided according to the definition of k-nearest neighbour weight matrices used ($k = 2$, 5 and 10, see Annex F for a definition of k-nearest neighbour weight matrices). The figures display the Moran's I statistic, which shows the degree of spatial correlation. Its value ranges from 1 (strong positive spatial autocorrelation) to –1 (strong negative spatial autocorrelation). The datasets are divided into the following four quadrants:

- The first quadrant (top left) associates low values of GDP (or GDP growth) with high values of GDP (or GDP growth) in neighbouring regions (LH).
- The second quadrant (top right) associates high values of GDP (or GDP growth) with high values of GDP (or GDP growth) (HH).
- The third quadrant (bottom right) associates high values of GDP (or GDP growth) with low values (HL) of GDP (or GDP growth).
- The fourth quadrant (bottom right) associates low values of GDP (or GDP growth) with low values (LL).

Figure 3.2-3.8 display a strong positive spatial correlation, and the correlation lessens when more neighbours are added (i.e. when k increases). The fact that values are more clustered in 2005 than in 1995 suggests there has been some convergence between neighbouring regions.

Spatial regressions

The spatial econometric regression uses the same model specifications as the cross-sectional and the panel models, with the addition of spatial components. The first regressor is the lagged dependent variable. If it is significant and positive it means that there is significant positive spatial correlation of the dependent variable. The spatial lag model is used here, that is the mixed regressive-spatial autoregressive (SAR) model (see Annex F for a detailed explanation):

$$y = \rho W_1 y + X\beta + \varepsilon$$
$$\varepsilon \sim N(0, \sigma^2 I_n) \tag{4}$$

The weight matrices used in equation 4 are $k = 2$, 5 and 10 (see Annex F for definitions and a deeper explanation).

Table 3.6. **Spatial results regional economic growth in OECD TL2 regions, 1995-2005**

	Model 1			Model 2			Model 3		
	k-2	k-5	k-10	k-2	k-5	k-10	k-2	k-5	k-10
Lagged Dependent	0.337	0.549	0.645	0.229	0.43	0.52	0.277	0.666	0.628
Variable	(7.226)**	(10.112)**	(10.77)**	(4.384)**	(6.733)**	(7.243)**	(4.891)**	(5.157)**	(8.89)**
Constant	0.017	0.016	0.015	0.126	0.103	0.1	0.134	0.143	0.084
	(1.936)	(1.933)	(1.766)	(7.427)**	(6.143)**	(5.802)**	(4.777)**	(4.78)**	(3.18)**
Initial Y	−0.0003	−0.0007	−0.0008	−0.008	−0.007	−0.007	−0.01	−0.01	−0.006
	(−0.38)	(−0.795)	(−0.911)	(−5.455)**	(−4.672)**	(−4.544)**	(−3.94)**	(−4.45)**	(−2.45)*
Infrast	–	–	–	0.012	0.013	0.014	0.015	0.02	0.015
				(1.937)	(2.225)*	(2.396)*	(2.216)*	(2.474)*	(2.24)*
Prim Ed	–	–	–	−0.01	−0.008	−0.008	−0.002	−0.003	−0.003
				(−8.565)**	(−7.114)**	(−6.7)**	(−3.183)**	(−3.116)**	(−3.144)**
Tert Ed	–	–	–	0.007	0.006	0.005	–	–	–
				(7.152)**	(5.808)**	(5.36)**			
Patents	–	–	–	–	–	–	0.001	0.001	0.0005
							(1.62)	(1.104)	(1.128)
R^2	0.262	0.362	0.336	0.407	0.464	0.46	0.309	0.232	0.411
Breusch-Pagan test	7.43	4.4	3.185	1.642	2.332	1.501	35.18	54	32.34
(p-value test)	0.006	0.036	0.074	0.801	0.675	0.826	0.00	0.00	0.00
n	333	333	333	274	274	274	232	232	232

*/ Significant at the 95% confidence level; **/ Significant at the 99% confidence level.
z-value in parentheses.
Source: Calculations based on *OECD Regional Database* (2008).

This coefficient finds that the performances of neighbouring regions strongly influences the performance of any given region in the OECD (Table 3.9), suggesting that inter-regional trade and inter-regional linkages play an important role in a region's performance.

This spatial correlation with growth also confirms that infrastructure and human capital are drivers of economic expansion, but it does not confirm previous results for innovation (Model 3). These results suggest that as capital and talent agglomerate they tend to positively influence growth in neighbouring regions, but innovation remains a highly local element that does not necessarily influence growth in neighbouring regions. It is also possible that our models should attempt to incorporate lagged values, as in our panel data analysis, at the same time that spatial econometrics is carried out.

Conclusions

In sum, this chapter reveals that regional growth depends on endogenous growth factors such as education and innovation, but also on infrastructure and on forces described by the NEG such as economies of agglomeration and geographic characteristics. The results show that policies can benefit from an integrated approach: polices aiming at providing infrastructure only are bound to be unsuccessful as endogenous growth factors such as human capital and innovation need also to be taken into account.

The dynamic panel model found that infrastructure and human capital require three years to positively influence regional growth, while innovation is a longer-term process, having a positive effect on regional growth only after a five-year period.

Our analysis based on a knowledge production function related innovation input variables such as human capital and R&D to innovation outcomes such as patenting activity. We found that i) human capital has a strong impact on regional growth both directly (from previous analysis), and indirectly, through patenting; ii) R&D is an indirect determinant of growth through its impact on patenting activity; and iii) geographical space plays a role in determining innovation in these models as agglomeration economies emerge as a determinant.

Our final analysis, spatial econometrics, found that the performance of neighbouring regions influences the performance of any given region in the OECD.

The main lessons from these results are that in order to promote regional growth, policy-makers should develop a comprehensive regional policy that not only links regions through infrastructure investments, but that also fosters human capital formation and facilitates the process of innovation. The risk of piecemeal visions of regional policy or of sectoral polices, such as only promoting human capital or only providing infrastructure, is that a "leaking" instead of a linking process will be created.

Notes

1. The term *economies of agglomeration* is used in *urban economics* to describe the benefits that firms obtain when locating near each other.

2. The basic proposition is that holding constant population expansion, and in the absence of technological progress, diminishing returns to scale will bring about convergence (Aghion and Howitt, 1998).

3. We defined the specialisation index as $Sp_i = \dfrac{Y_{ij}/Y_j}{Y_i/Y}$ where Y_{ij} is total employment of industry i in region j, Y_j is total employment in region j of all industries, Y_i is the national employment in industry i, and Y is the total national employment of all industries. A value of the index above 1 shows specialisation in an industry and a value below 1 shows non-specialisation.

4. We observe 16 regions as outliers in the data, mostly from Australia, Canada and Turkey, with a value of ln (distance to market) greater than 4.8.

5. Perhaps because they violate the Gauss-Markov assumptions used in regression modelling, i.e. that the distribution of the sample data exhibits a constant mean and variance as we move across observations.

ISBN 978-92-64-03945-2
How Regions Grow: Trends and Analysis
© OECD 2009

References

Aghion, P. and P. Howitt (1992), "A Model of Growth through Creative Destruction", *Econometrica*, Vol. 60. No. 2, pp. 323-51.

Aghion, P. and P. Howitt (1998), *Endogenous Growth Theory*, The MIT Press, Cambridge.

Arrow, K. (1962) "The Economic Implications of Learning by Doing", A *Review of Economic Studies*, Vol. 29, pp. 155-173.

Barro, R. (1997), *Determinants of Economic Growth*, MIT press.

Barro, R. and X. Sala-i Martin (1995), *Economic Growth*, New York, Mcgrew-Hill.

Becker, G. S. (1964, 1975 2nd edt.), *Human Capital*, New York, Columbia University Press.

Cass, D.(1965), "Optimum Growth in an Aggregative Model of Capital Accumulation", *The Review of Economic Studies*, Vol. 32, No. 3, pp. 233-240.

Crescenzi R. and A. Rodriguez-Pose (2006), "R&D, Spillovers, Innovation Systems and the Genesis of Regional Growth in Europe", ERSA conference papers ersa06p371, European Regional Science Association

Duranton, G. and D. Puga (2004), "Micro-foundations of Urban Agglomeration Economies,"*Handbook of Regional and Urban Economics*, in: J. V. Henderson and J. F. Thisse (ed.), Handbook of Regional and Urban Economics, Edition 1, Vol. 4, Chapter 48, pp. 2063-2117.

Englmann, F.C. and U. Walz (1995), "Industrial Centers and Regional Growth in the Presence of Local Inputs", *Journal of Regional Science*, Vol. 35, No. 1, pp. 3-27.

Fujita, M., Krugman, P. and A. J. Venables (1999), *The Spatial Economy: Cities, Regions and International Trade.* pp. 25-42.

Grossman, G. and E. Helpman (1994), "Endogenous Innovation in the Theory of Growth", *Journal of Economic Perspectives*, Vol. 8, No. 1, pp. 23-44.

Hirschman, A.O. (1958), *The Strategy of Economic Development.* New Haven, CT: Yale University Press.

Kaldor, N. (1957), "A Model of Economic Growth", *The Economic Journal*, Vol. 67, No. 268, pp. 591-624.

Koopmans, Tjalling C. (1965), "On the Concept of Optimal Economic Growth," in (Study Week on the) Econometric Approach to Development Planning, Chap. 4, pp. 225–87. North-Holland Publishing Co., Amsterdam.

Krugman, P. (1991), "Increasing Returns and Economic Geography", *The Journal of Political Economy*, Vol. 99, No. 3, pp. 483-99.

Krugman, P. and A.J. Venables (1995), "Globalization and the Inequality of Nations", *Quarterly Journal of Economics*, Vol. 110, No. 4, pp. 857-880.

Krugman, P. and A.J. Venables (1996), "Integration, Specialization, and Adjustment", *European Economic Review*, Vol. 40, pp. 959-67.

Lucas R.E. (1988), "On the Mechanics of Economic Development", *Journal of Monetary Economics*, No. 22, pp. 3-42.

Martin, P. and G.I.P. Ottaviano (2001), "Growth and Agglomeration", *International Economic Review,* Vol. 42, No. 4, pp. 947-68.

Myrdal, G. (1957), *Economic Theory and Underdeveloped Regions*, London: Duckworth.

Nelson R. and E. Phelps (1966), "Investment in Humans, Technological Diffusion and Economic Growth", *American Economic Review*, No. 61, pp. 69-75.

OECD (2009), *Regions at a Glance.*

Perroux, F. (1955), "Note sur la Notion de Pôle de Croissance", *Économie Appliquée*, No. 8, pp. 307-320.

Puga, D. (1999), "The Rise and Fall of Regional Inequalities", *European Economic Review* Vol. 43, pp. 303-34.

Puga, D. (1998), "Urbanization Patterns: European Versus Less Developed Countries", *Journal of Regional Science*, Vol. 38, No. 2, pp. 231-52.

Puga, D. and A.J. Venables (1996), "The Spread of Industry: Spatial Agglomeration in Economic Development", *Journal of Japanese and International Economies*, Vol. 10, pp. 440-64.

Puga, D. and A.J. Venables (1997), "Preferential Trading Arrangements and Industrial Location", *Journal of International Economics*, Vol. 43, pp. 347-68.

Ramsey F.P. (1928), "A Mathematical Theory of Saving", *Economic Journal*, Vol. 38, No. 152, pp. 543-559.

Rebelo, S. (1991). "Long-Run Policy Analysis and Long-Run Growth,"*Journal of Political Economy*, Vol. 99, No. 3, pp. 500-521.

Romer, P. M. (1986), "Increasing Returns and Long-run Growth", *Journal of Political Economy*, Vol. 94, No. 5, pp. 1002-37.

Romer, P. M. (1987), "Growth Based on Increasing Returns Due to Specialization", *American Economic Review*, Vol. 77, No. 2, pp. 56-62.

Romer, P. M. (1990), "Endogenous Technical Change", *Journal of Political Economy*, Vol. 99, pp. 72-102.

Sheshkinski, E. (1967), Tests of the Learning by Doing' Hypothesis, *Review of Economics and Statistics*, No. 49, pp. 568–78.

Solow, R. (1956). "A Contribution to the Theory of Economic Growth", *Quarterly Journal of Economics*, Vol. 70, pp. 65-94.

Spiezia V. and S. Weiler (2007), "Understanding Regional Growth", *The Review of Regional Studies* Vol. 37, No. 3, pp. 344-366.

Swan, T. (1956), "Economic Growth and Capital Accumulation", *Economic Record*, Vol. 32, pp. 343-61.

Uzawa H. (1965), "Optimal Technical Change in an Aggregate Model of Economic Growth", *International Economic Review*, Vol. 6, pp. 18-31.

Venables, A. (1996), "Equilibrium Locations of Vertically Linked Industries", *International Economic Review*, Vol. 37, No. 2, pp. 341-59.

Williamson, J.G. (1965), "Regional Inequalities and the Process of National Development", *Economic Development and Cultural Change*, Vol. 13, pp. 1-84.

ISBN 978-92-64-03945-2
How Regions Grow: Trends and Analysis
© OECD 2009

ANNEX A

The Components of Regional Growth

Average productivity

Due to availability of data, average productivity at the regional level is defined by GDP per worker, where employment is measured at place of work. A rise in the regional share of GDP may be due to rapid growth – relative to the country's growth rate – in average productivity. Average productivity, in turn, depends on technology, labour skills, production capital and infrastructure. All of these factors can be mobilised through regional infrastructure investment policies, through education and training to promote higher skill levels; and through research and innovation to create more efficient production technology. Therefore, the proportion of regional growth that is due to growth in average productivity tends to be based on regional assets.

A rise in the GDP share of a region may also be due to specialisation (in sectors with fast growth in GDP per worker) or to a change in specialisation towards sectors with high GDP per worker. Specialisation is a result of a region's comparative advantages, which depend on both irreproducible (e.g. land, oil) and reproducible inputs (e.g. skills, capital). The proportion of regional GDP growth due to specialisation based on irreproducible inputs can be attributed to natural endowments. However, unlike the stock of irreproducible inputs that is fixed, skills can be upgraded through education and training, and capital can be accumulated through investments. Therefore, the proportion of regional growth due to specialisation based on reproducible inputs can be regarded as a function of regional assets.

The labour market

High growth in employment rates may be due to higher skill levels (skilled workers have higher employment rates than unskilled ones) or to greater efficiency of the local labour market, e.g. regulations and institutions which enable a better match between labour supply and demand. Both can be regarded as resulting from regional assets: skills can be upgraded through

107

training and education, and changes in employment regulations and labour institutions can increase the efficiency of the regional labour market.

A relative rise in activity rates may be the result of an increase in the working-age population or of an increase in participation rates across all age groups. Higher rates of growth of the working-age population may either follow natural demographic trends or be due to policies to attract working-age migrants from other regions and countries. Therefore, a rise in activity rates due to natural demographic trends can be seen as resulting from natural endowments. In contrast, an increase in the working-age population via migration and higher participation rates across all age groups are indicators of regional assets.

Population

Finally, higher rates of population growth may either follow natural demographic trends or be due to policies to attract migrants from other regions and countries.

ISBN 978-92-64-03945-2
How Regions Grow: Trends and Analysis
© OECD 2009

ANNEX B

Methodology for Decomposition of Factors of Growth

The share of region i in the total GDP of the OECD can be written as:

$$\frac{GDP_i}{GDP_{OECD}} = \frac{GDP_j}{GDP_{OECD}} * \frac{GDP_i}{GDP_j} \tag{1}$$

where j denotes the country of region i. The GDP share of region i in country j is then equal to:

$$\frac{GDP_i}{GDP_j} = \frac{GDP_i / E_i}{GDP_j / E_j} * \frac{E_i / LF_i}{E_j / LF_j} * \frac{LF_i / WA_i}{LF_j / WA_j} * \frac{WA_i / P_i}{WA_j / P_j} * \frac{P_i}{P_j} \tag{2}$$

where P, E, LF and WA stand, respectively, for population, employment, labour force and working age (15-64) population. Therefore the GDP share of region i in country j is a function of its productivity, employment rate, participation rate, age-activity rate and population, relative to, respectively, the productivity, employment rate, participation rate, age-activity rate and population of its country defined as the following:

- Productivity is defined as GDP per worker (GDP/E), where employment is measured at the place of work.

- The employment rate is defined as the percent of labour force that is employed (E/LF), where the labour force is the number of employed plus the number of unemployed.

- The participation rate is the ratio between the labour force and the working age population (LF/WA), where the working age population comprises the ages 15 to 64.

- The activity rate is the population in the working age class (ages 15 to 64) as a per cent of the total population.

109

By substituting equation 2 into equation 1, taking the logarithm and differentiating it, one obtains:

1. $(g_i - g_i) = (g_{p,i} - g_{p,i}) + (g_{e,i} - g_{e,i}) + (g_{lf,i} - g_{lf,i}) + (g_{wa,i} - g_{wa,i}) + (g_{p,i} - g_{p,i}) (3)$

or, equivalently

| Difference in GDP growth between region i and the country j | = | Growth difference in GDP per worker between region i and country j | + | Growth difference in the employment rate between region i and country j | + | Growth difference in the participation rate between region i and country j | + | Growth difference in the activity rate between region i and country j | + | Growth difference in population between region i and country j |

ISBN 978-92-64-03945-2
How Regions Grow: Trends and Analysis
© OECD 2009

ANNEX C

Summary of Neoclassical and Endogenous Growth Models

Table C.1. **Summary table: growth theories**

Neo-classical growth models		
Model	Assumptions/Premises	Prediction
Ramsey (1928)	• Homogenous goods • Constant preferences and population • Innovation is reflected in wealth accumulation	Utility function that determines savings and wealth accumulation
Solow (1956) and Swan (1956)	• Diminishing returns to capital and labour • Constant return to scale productions function • Constant savings rate	Convergence of countries depending on their steady-state level which in turn is conditional on savings, population growth and the production function. Diminishing returns to capital imply that in the absence of technological change, growth would stop. As empirically long-run growth does not stop, technological progress was assumed to be exogenous.
Cass (1965) and Koopmans (1965)	• Saving rate is endogenously determined. • Constant returns to scale • No external sector • Homogeneous outputs and factors • Diminishing marginal rate of substitution • Positive marginal productivities • Population and labour grow constantly and are exogenous.	Absolute convergence. If all countries have the same steady-state income path, then differences in initial income will represent different positions with respect to the common steady-state, and hence the faster the growth rate.

Table C.1. **Summary table: growth theories** (cont.)

Neo-classical growth models

Endogenous Growth Models

Model	Assumptions/Premises	Prediction
Arrow (1962) and Sheshinski (1967)	• Differences in types of capital (new capital being preferred to old one) • Constant returns to scale • Learning, a process of acquiring knowledge is endogenous to the model • Only one capital-labour ratio is optimum • Learning only takes place in the capital sector, no learning occurs once the capital good is created and is being used. • Learning is a by-product of production instead of a product of a learning system (based on universities for instance) • Knowledge is non-rival.	Discoveries immediately spillover to the entire economy as knowledge is non-rival
Romer (1986) Lucas (1988)	• Knowledge is an input of production • Knowledge displays increasing marginal productivity • Increasing returns to scale • Decreasing returns in the production of new knowledge • Knowledge produces externalities.	Competitive assumptions can be maintained and determines an equilibrium rate of technological progress but the growth rate is not Pareto optimal. At the end, growth and knowledge can increase boundlessly. No convergence is predicted.
Romer (1987, 1990) Aghion and Howitt (1992)	• Imperfect competition • Technological change arises from intentional decisions from profit-maximising agents. • Technology is a non-rival partially excludable good.	R&D activities reward firms through monopolistic power. The equilibrium is not Pareto optimal, but rather one with monopolistic competition. The stock of human capital determines growth, but too little human capital will be devoted to R&D. Also, integration into world markets increases growth rates, and large populations are not sufficient to generate growth.

ISBN 978-92-64-03945-2
How Regions Grow: Trends and Analysis
© OECD 2009

ANNEX D

Main Models of the New Economic Geography

Krugman's 1991 model includes two *a priori* identical regions in endowment factors; two factors of production – agriculture with its constant-returns tied to the land, and manufacturers with increasing-returns (though a monopolistic Dixit-Stiglitz model) – that can be located in each region; and transportation costs for manufacturing goods. Workers are mobile across regions. The model finds that as transportation costs decrease and economies of large-scale production are present, a region with a relatively large non-rural population (or larger initial production) will be an attractive place to produce because of the large local market and because of the availability of goods and services produced there. This will attract more people increasing local demand and profits and attracting more firms. The forces of agglomeration depend on the level of trade cost and the proportion of mobile population in response to wage differentials. The external economies are pecuniary (not technological), arising from the desirability of selling to and buying from a region in which other producers are concentrated.

Krugman extends his 1991 model to examine equilibrium locations in continuous space. This model (1993), built with the same assumptions as the 1991 model, is geared for explaining the formation of metropolitan centres. The analysis finds that agglomeration holds population concentration together and allows this concentration to occur in a variety of possible sites. Thus there are multiple equilibria for a metropolitan location.

Krugman and Venables (1995) drop the assumption of labour mobility. This model contains two economies (regions) identical in endowment preferences and technology, and two factors of production: agriculture and manufacturing. The manufacturing sector has monopolistic increasing returns to scale (Dixit-Stiglitz) and produces final goods as well as intermediate goods. The manufacturing sector has constant returns. The model assumes transportation costs. At high transportation costs all regions have the same manufacturing production. When transportation costs fall

113

below a critical value the region with the larger (initial) manufacturing share will attract more firms due to forward and backward industrial linkages:

● Producers of final goods will find larger industrial concentration more attractive because there is a larger base of intermediate producers, giving rise to forward (cost) linkages.

● Producers of intermediate goods will find it advantageous to produce near the large final good industry, giving rise to backward (demand) linkages.

These forward and backward linkages will increase the real income of the core region relative to the periphery. If costs, however, continue to fall further, the wage differential will induce firms to relocate back to peripheral regions.

In **Venables (1996)** each economy has three sectors. The first sector (perfectly competitive) produces a tradeable good. The other two are monopolistically competitive and vertically linked, one providing an intermediate good to the other. Each industry contains firms in two locations and all firms supply to both locations. The production decision depends on the level of linkages and transportation costs. When transportation costs are high, firms locate close to consumers and thus produce in both locations. When transportation costs are low, firms also produce in both locations, bringing convergence since factor prices are low. For intermediate transportation costs clustering forces come to dominate giving rise to multiple equilibria. Some industries will agglomerate while others may spread out in response to factor price differences.

Krugman and Venables (1996) extend Venables (1996) by studying the process of European integration. This model includes two industries in two countries (regions). Both industries produce final and intermediate goods and use intermediate goods for production. Their technology of production is characterised by increasing monopolistic returns to scale. There is no labour mobility and transportation costs are present. This simple model can be extended to study the dynamics of economic integration between several countries, each containing a variety of industries. The model starts with high transportation costs. Countries in this case will maintain the full range of industries since backward and forward linkages are not strong enough to lead to agglomeration. For very low transportation costs, the country with a strong initial position in some industry finds itself with an advantage that culminates over time due to forward and backward linkages. Each industry will completely concentrate in one country. For the intermediate value of transportation, agglomeration will take place only if industries are initially very unequally distributed.

Puga and Venables (1996) build a model for representing the process of industrialisation. In their model there are N identical countries producing manufacturing (with increasing returns) and agricultural goods (with constant returns). Trade/transportation costs are present while labour is immobile. The agglomeration forces are input-output linkages between firms in the industrial sector. If these forces are strong enough industry will concentrate in a single country. Wages in this country will be higher than elsewhere but the positive pecuniary externality will compensate for the higher wage costs until a critical mass is reached. At this point it becomes profitable for some industries to move out of this country into another country. More firms eventually move into this country to benefit from the backward and forward linkages, raising wages in this country until a critical mass is reached. The model predicts industrial spillover through a series of waves, from one country to another. Thus only a few countries are industrialised even if countries are identical to each other in their underlying structure.

In **Englemann and Waltz (1995)** there are two regions and four goods: a traditional good produced by skilled and unskilled labour, an industrial commodity, a sector producing non-tradable local goods and services, and a research and development sector. Mobile households supply skilled labour and immobile households supply unskilled labour. Both regions have identical monopolistic production functions. Growth is based on endogenous technological change in the non-traded sector. The model considers two extreme cases. The first assumes knowledge spillovers in research and development which only occur locally. In this case a core-periphery pattern always emerges where the region with a higher initial number of intermediates becomes the only industrial centre. The second extreme case assumes perfect interregional knowledge spillover effects, where knowledge is transported through the mobility of workers and the free tradeability of the industrial good containing the newly developed intermediate goods. This case allows for a variety of possible solutions (depending on the parameter values). These solutions comprise a stable steady state equilibrium with equal growth rates in both regions, even if one region is relatively specialised in the industrial good and the traditional sector is completely concentrated in the other region.

Martin and Ottaviano (2001) merge the NEG with endogenous growth models. Their model includes two regions, each region endowed with a fixed amount of labour assumed to be immobile across regions. Transaction costs are present. A composite good is produced by a homogenous (constant returns) and a differentiated good (monopolistic production technology). The composite good can be used as intermediate input in the innovation sector to create new varieties of the composite good, thus innovation and production are jointly determined. The blueprint of the good is protected infinitely by a patent whose initial property belongs to the region where invention has taken place. The innovation sector is perfectly competitive. Patents can be sold and are initially equally distributed among regions. The equilibria in the model yield two solutions. If the economy starts in equilibrium there is no incentive to relocate production of the increasing returns sector because the demands for differentiated goods as well as their profits are the same in both regions. If one region gets more firms producing differentiated goods, then the cost of inputs for innovation in that region will be lower due to the presence of transaction cost between the regions. Agglomeration will occur in the region where all the innovation activity has developed. The other region will cease any innovation activity.

Puga (1998a) develops a model similar to Krugman (1991) for exploring why urbanisation patterns in Europe are different than in the less developed countries. The model includes two regions, each allowing for a possible city and agricultural hinterland location. There are transportation costs, labour migration, and two sectors; manufacturing with increasing returns, and agriculture with constant returns. The novelty relative to Krugman (1991) is in allowing for labour mobility between both sectors. With this modification, the elasticity of labour supply is also a pecuniary externality in addition to internal economies of scales in manufacturing and the cost of spatial interactions which encourages firms and workers to choose locations with good market access (which in turn are locations with many firms and workers). Agglomeration is enhanced in the emerging city when labour supply is sufficiently elastic, since labour can be drawn from other cities and from the pool of agricultural workers. Under high transportation costs, the model predicts the emergence of a balanced system of cities. When transportation costs are low, agglomeration forces lead to urban primacy. A high elasticity of labour supply enhances the development of a primate urban pattern. Puga concludes that the larger metropolises present in the less developed countries are due to lower costs of spatial interaction, stronger economies of scale, and more elasticity in supply of labour to the urban centre.

Puga (1999) notes salient differences in patterns of economic geography between Europe and the US. In the latter there are narrower income differentials and a higher concentration of industry. The model in this paper addresses whether integration in Europe will narrow the differences relative to the US, or augment them. The model includes two regions, each with increasing returns in the manufacturing sector and constant returns in the agricultural sector. There are transportation costs, mobility between sectors, and backward and forward firm linkages. The model is divided into two specifications. In the first, labour is also mobile between regions, and in the second it is fixed (but mobile between sectors). The first specification adds forward and backward linkages and intersectoral migration to Krugman's (1991) model. The results obtained in Krugman's model also hold with these additions: high trade costs yield convergence (no agglomeration), and reductions in trade costs beyond a threshold level yield agglomeration. In the second specification (no interregional migration) firms split between the regions at high trade costs. At intermediate levels of trade they agglomerate due to cost and demand linkages creating wage differentials. At low levels of trade cost firms spread out across regions again since they want to be where immobile factors are cheaper. Thus for the case of European integration (a reduction in trade costs) agglomeration depends on the mobility of labour. If labour is mobile, agglomeration will be intensified. If on the other hand it is not mobile, agglomeration will occur, but eventually firms will spread out across regions in response to the wage differentials.

ISBN 978-92-64-03945-2
How Regions Grow: Trends and Analysis
© OECD 2009

ANNEX E

Distance and Accessibility

Measures of distance

Simple accessibility indicators consider only intra-regional transport infrastructure expressed by measures of motorway length, number of railway stations or travel time to the nearest nodes of interregional networks. More complex accessibility indicators take into account the connectivity of transport networks by distinguishing between the network itself, *i.e.* its nodes and links, and the "activities" (such as work, shopping or leisure) or "opportunities" (such as markets or jobs) that can be reached by it. In general terms accessibility can be constructed using two separate functions, one representing the activities or opportunities to be reached and the other representing the effort, time, distance or cost needed to reach them:

$$A_i = \Sigma_j \, g(W_j) \, f(c_{ij}) \tag{1}$$

where:

- A_i is the accessibility of region i,
- $g(W_j)$ is the activity W to be reached in region j, and
- $f(c_{ij})$ is the generalised cost of reaching region j from region i.

The functions $g(W_j)$ and $f(c_{ij})$ are called *activity functions* and *impedance functions*, respectively. They are associated multiplicatively, *i.e.* they are weights to each other. W_j is the accumulated total of the activities reachable at j weighted by the ease of getting from i to j. This general index is of a gravitational type where the attractors are the activities or opportunities in regions j (including region i itself), and the distance term is the impedance.

This means that the greater the number of attractive destinations in regions j and the more accessible regions j are from region i, the greater is the accessibility of region i. This definition of accessibility is referred to as destination-oriented accessibility. In a similar way an origin-oriented accessibility can be defined as following: the more people live in regions j and the more easily they can visit region i, the greater is the accessibility of region

i. Because of the symmetry of most transport connections, destination-oriented and origin-oriented accessibility tend to be highly correlated. Different types of accessibility indicators can be constructed by specifying different forms of functions (Table E.1).

Table E.1. **Typology of accessibility indices**

Type of accessibility	Activity function $g(W_j)$	Impedance function $f(c_{ij})$
Travel cost Accumulated travel cost to a set of activities	$W_j \mid 1$ if $W_j^* \geq W_{min}$ 0 if $W_j < W_{min}$	c_{ij}
Daily accessibility Accumulated activities in a given travel time	W_j	1 if $c_{ij} \leq c_{max}$ 0 if $c_{ij} > c_{max}$
Potential Accumulated activities weighted by a function of travel cost	W_j^{α}	$\exp(-\beta c_{ij})$

The European Planning Observation Network (ESPON) project developed a GIS database and a set of peripherality indicators for all European regions down to NUTS3 level using the *potential* category as the type of accessibility indicator. This indicator assumes that the attraction of a destination increases with size (activity function) and declines with distance or travel time or cost (impedance function):

● The activity function may be linear or non-linear and is usually represented by regional population, regional GDP, or total income. Occasionally the attraction term W_j is weighted by an exponent greater than one to take account of agglomeration effects, *i.e.* the fact that larger facilities may be disproportionally more attractive than smaller ones.

● The impedance function is nonlinear. Generally a negative exponential function is used in which a larger parameter β indicates that nearby destinations are given greater weight than remote ones.

Potential accessibility indicators are superior to travel time accessibility indicators and daily accessibility indicators in that they are founded on sound behavioural principles of stochastic utility maximisation. Their disadvantage is that they contain parameters that need to be calibrated and that their values cannot be easily interpreted in familiar units such as travel time or number of people one can reach. Therefore potential indicators are frequently expressed in per cent of average accessibility of all regions or, if changes of accessibility are studied, in per cent of average accessibility of all regions in the base year of the comparison.

From the above three basic accessibility indicators, an almost unlimited variety of derivative indicators can be developed. The most important ones are multimodal, intermodal and interoperable accessibility. In all three cases the equations given above remain valid. What changes is the way transport cost c_{ij} is calculated. All three types of accessibility indicator can be calculated for any mode. On a European scale, accessibility indicators for road, rail and air are most frequently calculated, as well as multimodal indicators. Differences between modes are usually expressed by using different "generalised" cost functions such as:

$$c_{ijm} = v_m t_{ijm} + c_m d_{ijm} + u_m k_{ijm} \tag{2}$$

where: t_{ijm}, d_{ijm} and k_{ijm} are travel time, travel distance and convenience of travel from location i to destinations j by mode m, respectively, and v_m, c_m and u_m are value of time, cost per kilometre and inconvenience of mode m, respectively. In addition there may be a fixed travel cost component as well as cost components taking account of network access at either end of a trip such as waiting and transfer times at stations, waiting times at borders or congestion in metropolitan areas.

Measuring distance to markets and accessibility to markets in OECD regions

In this section we develop two measures of accessibility (travel cost and potential in Table E.1) using the general equation (1). Our first sets of indicators provide a measure of **distance to markets** by defining the activity and impedance functions in the equation as follows:

$$g(Wj) = GDP \tag{3}$$

$$f(c_{ij}) = c_{ij} \tag{4}$$

where:

c_{ij} in (4) is the simple linear distance between region centroids i and j.

In this specification the higher the index, the higher will be the "marginality" of region i (because distance enters linearly) or, put another way, the more distant will be this region to the markets (keeping GDP constant).

Our second indicators measure **accessibility to markets** by defining the activity and impedance function as:

$$g(Wj) = GDP \tag{5}$$

$$f(c_{ij}) = exp(-\beta c_{ij}) \tag{6}$$

where

β in A16 is set at the value 0.05 and

c_{ij} in (6) is the simple linear distance between region centroids i and j.

The negative exponential function in (6) gives decreasing weight to more distant regions (i.e. the more distant the region, the less weight it will have), providing a measure of "local accessibility" or access to the main "near" markets.

This measure is heavily influenced by the size of regions: the larger the area of a region, the higher will be the distance between its centroid and the centroid of other regions. As a consequence, the larger the area of a region, the further the region will be from markets (as proxied by other regions' GDP). In order to partly obviate this undesirable feature, we assigned a distance of zero to bordering regions.*

Both indices are expressed as a percentage of the average index of the economic area under study. We consider two types of economic areas as measures for markets:

● The entire OECD area as a single economic area.

● The OECD area partitioned into four regional economic or market blocks: North America, Europe, Japan and Korean, and Oceania.

Our measures have two main drawbacks: first, they do not account for travel time and transportation networks and modes; and second, our measures are heavily affected by the size of TL2 regions (despite the adjustment for bordering regions). Figures E1 to E8 display all four indices.

---

* Mathematically this means setting $c_{ij} = 0$ in (6) and $c_{ij} = 1$ in (4) so that the contribution of bordering regions will be their GDP.

Figure E.1. **Distance to markets**
Total OECD area

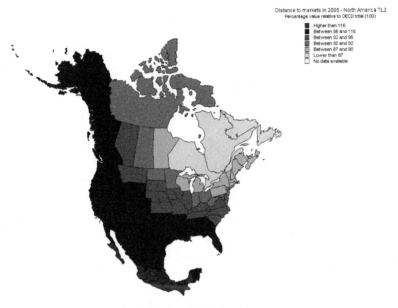

By blocks – North America

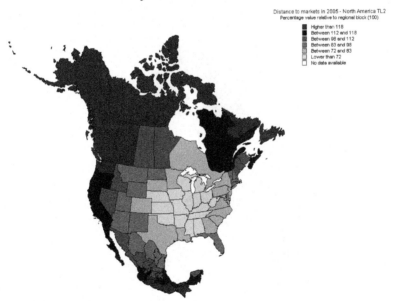

Note: The higher the value the more distant a region is to markets.

Figure E.2. **Distance to markets, Europe**
Total OECD area

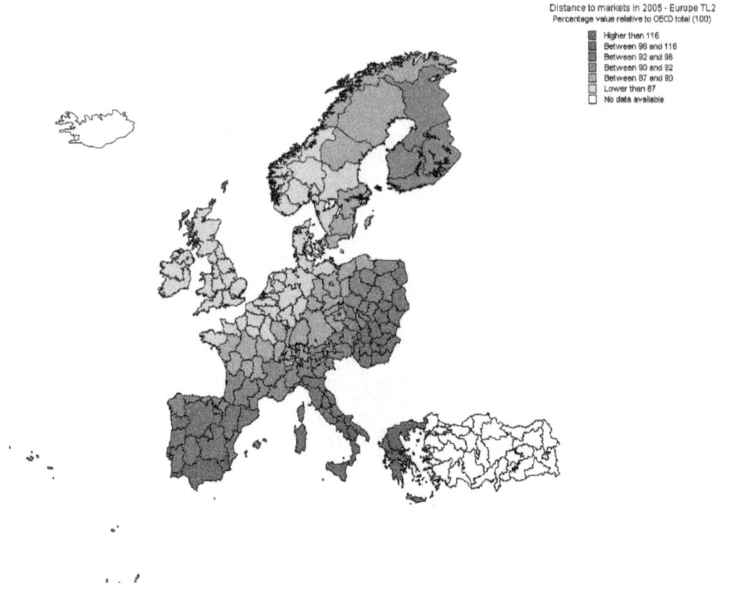

Distance to markets in 2005 - Europe TL2
Percentage value relative to OECD total (100)

- Higher than 116
- Between 96 and 116
- Between 92 and 96
- Between 90 and 92
- Between 87 and 90
- Lower than 87
- No data available

By blocks – Europe

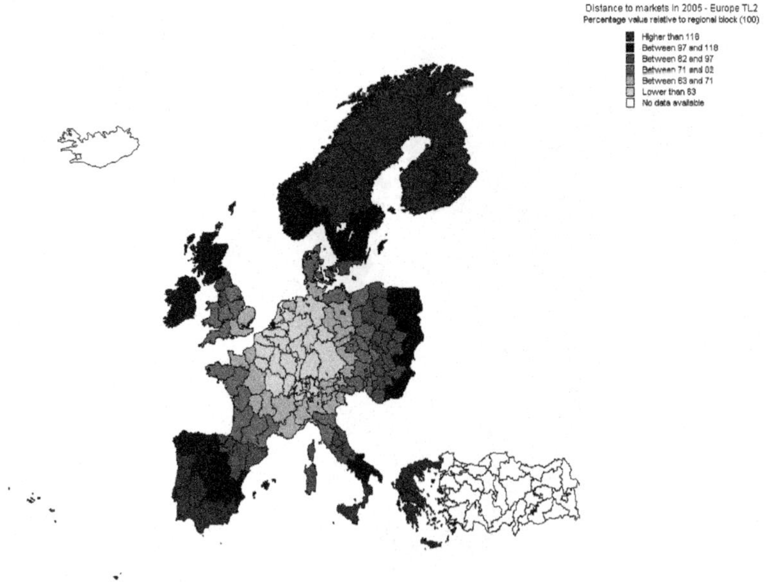

Distance to markets in 2005 - Europe TL2
Percentage value relative to regional block (100)

- Higher than 118
- Between 97 and 118
- Between 82 and 97
- Between 71 and 82
- Between 63 and 71
- Lower than 63
- No data available

Note: The higher the value the more distant a region is to markets.

Figure E.3. **Distance to markets, Japan and Korea**
Total OECD area

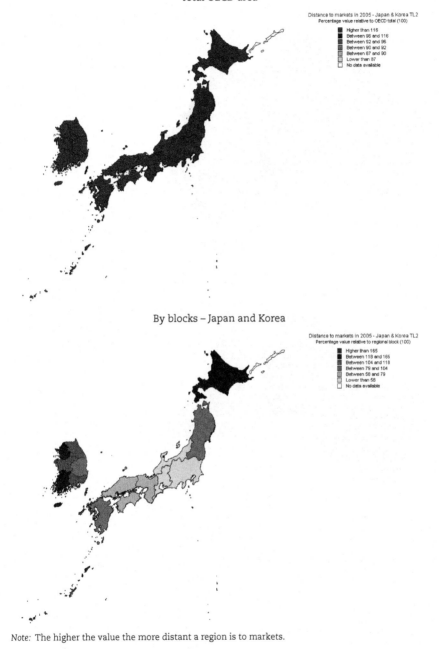

Distance to markets in 2005 - Japan & Korea TL2
Percentage value relative to OECD total (100)

- Higher than 116
- Between 96 and 116
- Between 92 and 96
- Between 90 and 92
- Between 87 and 90
- Lower than 87
- No data available

By blocks – Japan and Korea

Distance to markets in 2005 - Japan & Korea TL2
Percentage value relative to regional block (100)

- Higher than 165
- Between 118 and 165
- Between 104 and 118
- Between 79 and 104
- Between 58 and 79
- Lower than 58
- No data available

Note: The higher the value the more distant a region is to markets.

Figure E.4. **Distance to markets, Oceania**
Total OECD area

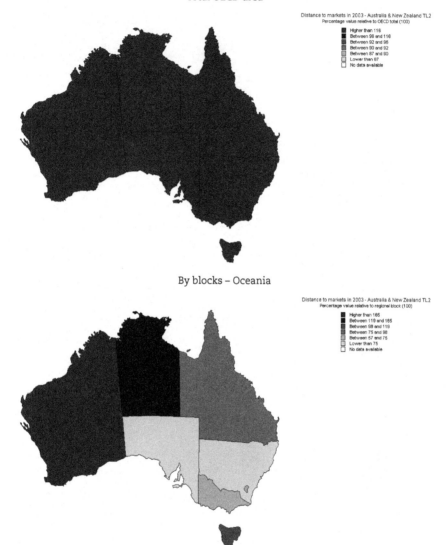

By blocks – Oceania

Note: The higher the value the more distant a region is to markets.

Figure E.5. **Access to markets, North America**

Total OECD area

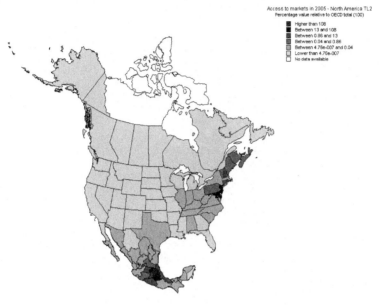

By blocks – North America

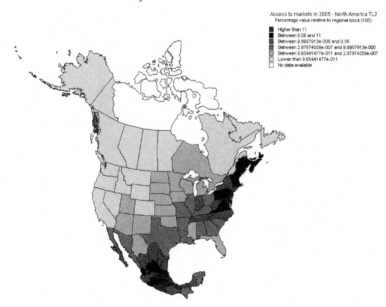

Note: The higher the value the better access the region has to markets.

Figure E.6. **Access to markets, Europe**
Total OECD area

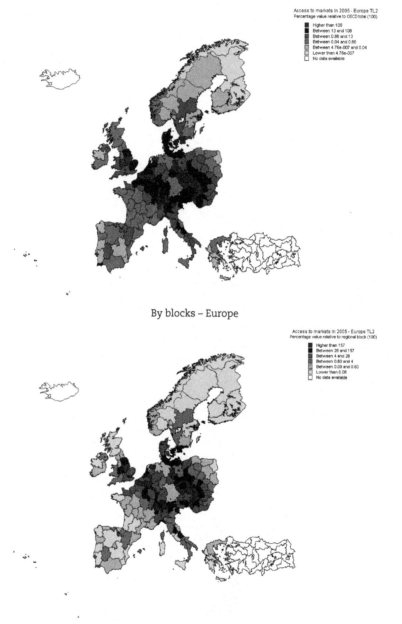

Note: The higher the value the better access the region has to markets.

Figure E.7. **Access to markets, Japan and Korea**
Total OECD area

Access to markets in 2003 - Japan & Korea TL2
Percentage value relative to OECD total (100)

- Higher than 108
- Between 13 and 108
- Between 0.86 and 13
- Between 0.04 and 0.86
- Between 4.76e-007 and 0.04
- Lower than 4.76e-007
- No data available

By blocks – Japan and Korea

Access to markets in 2005 - Japan & Korea TL2
Percentage value relative to regional block (100)

- Higher than 375
- Between 97 and 375
- Between 5 and 97
- Between 1 and 5
- Between 1.03149951e-005 and 1
- Lower than 1.03149951e-005
- No data available

Note: The higher the value the better access the region has to markets.

Figure E.8. **Access to markets, Oceania**
Total OECD area

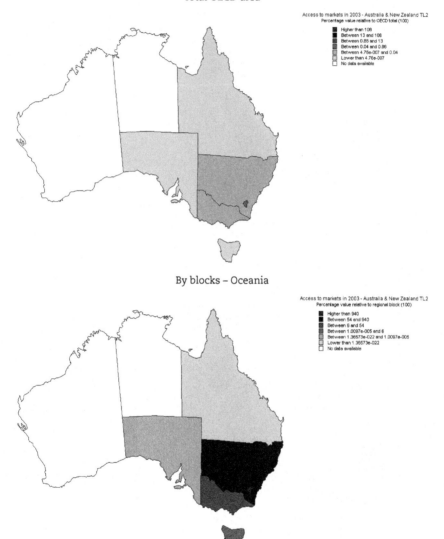

Note: The higher the value the better access the region has to markets.

ISBN 978-92-64-03945-2
How Regions Grow: Trends and Analysis
© OECD 2009

ANNEX F

Spatial Econometrics

Types of spatial data

i) *Point* or *georeferenced* data, where each point in space has a unique spatial identifier (*e.g.* longitude and latitude coordinates) and where the vector of observations is random and varies continuously over a fixed space. This is often referred to as *geostatistical* data. We thus have a continuous fixed space where the location of each data point is random.

ii) *Point pattern data*, similar to georeferenced data but where the space is also random. Such datasets are, for example, used to count events and their clustering.

iii) *Areal* (or *lattice*) data, where the space (of a regular or irregular shape) is fixed but partitioned into a finite number of areal units with well-defined boundaries, for example census (or other administrative) tracts.

Spatial statistics

To detect spatial patterns (association and autocorrelation), some standard global and local spatial statistics have been developed. These include Moran's I, Geary's C, G statistics, LISA and GLISA. All these techniques have two things in common: they start from the assumption of a spatially random distribution of data, and the spatial pattern and structure and the form of spatial dependence are typically derived from the data. The most common measure of spatial correlation is Moran's I. This index is analogous to the correlation coefficient, and its value ranges from 1 (strong positive spatial autocorrelation) to –1 (strong negative spatial autocorrelation). It is often used to measure the spatial autocorrelation of ordinal, interval or ratio data. Moran's I is defined by

$$I(d) = \frac{\sum_{i}^{n}\sum_{j\neq i}^{n} w_{ij}\left(x_i - \bar{x}\right)\left(x_j - \bar{x}\right)}{S^2 \sum_{i}^{n}\sum_{j\neq i}^{n} w_{ij}}$$

(1)

131

where, $S^2 = \frac{1}{n}\sum_i^n (x_i - \bar{x})^2$ i.e. the variance of x_i, which denotes the observed value of population at location i, $\bar{x}$ is the average of the x_i over the n locations, and w_{ij} is the spatial weight measure of contiguity, equal to 1 if i is contiguous to j, and equal to 0 otherwise (see spatial weight matrices below). It is therefore clear that the result of the test is based upon the postulated spatial structure reflected in the weights w_{ij}. Thus the elements of the spatial weight matrix W are exogenous and non-stochastic to the model. The expected value and variance of the Moran's I for a sample of size n could be calculated according to the assumed pattern of the spatial data distribution. For the assumption of a normal distribution:

$$E_n(I) = -\frac{1}{n-1} \quad \text{and} \quad V_n(I) = \frac{n^2 w_1 - n w_2 + 3 w_0^2}{w_0^2 (n^2 - 1)} - E_n^2(I) \tag{2}$$

For the assumption of a random distribution:

$$E_r(I) = -\frac{1}{n-1} \quad \text{and} \quad V_r(I) = \frac{n\left(\left(n^2 - 3n + 3\right)w_1 - n w_2 + 3 w_0^2\right) - K_2\left(\left(n^2 - n\right)w_1 - 2n w_2 + 6 w_0^2\right)}{w_0^2 (n-1)(n-2)(n-3)} - E_r^2(I) \tag{3}$$

where $K_2 = \frac{n \sum_i^n (x_i - \bar{x})^4}{\left(\sum_i^n (x_i - \bar{x})^2\right)^2}$, $w_0 = \sum_i^n \sum_j^n w_{ij}$, $w_1 = \frac{1}{2}\sum_i^n \sum_j^n (w_{ij} + w_{ji})^2$ and $w_2 =$, and where $w_{i\bullet}$ and $w_{\bullet i}$ are the sums of the row i and the column i of the weight matrix, respectively.

The test of the null, that there is no spatial autocorrelation between observed values over the n locations, can be done on the basis of the following standardised statistics:

$$Z(d) = \frac{I(d) - E(I)}{\sqrt{V(I)}} \tag{4}$$

Moran's I is significant and positive when the observed values of locations within a certain distance d tend to be similar, negative when they tend to be dissimilar, and approximately zero when the observed values are arranged randomly and independently over space.

The results of Moran's I and other spatial tests should be interpreted with caution. First, the choice of neighbours and their respective weights determines the values of the statistics. A non-significant result indicates that there is no significant spatial autocorrelation given the neighbourhood structure provided. Second, a significant positive autocorrelation could be caused by a spatial pattern in the data not specified by the statistical model. This model misspecification can be controlled for by incorporating a spatial weight matrix into the statistical model.

HOW REGIONS GROW: TRENDS AND ANALYSIS – ISBN 978-92-64-03945-2 – © OECD 2009

There are also asymptotic approaches for testing whether spatial correlation is present in the residuals from an OLS regression model. Some of these are the Likelihood Ratio (LR), the Wald and the Lagrange Multiplier (LM) tests, all based on maximum likelihood estimation.

Spatial weight matrices based on contiguity

Contiguity is modelled through a binary matrix W, whose elements take a value of 1 if two units are "neighbours" and 0 if they are not. For example, the element a_{12} (row 1, column 2) of W will have a value of 1 if regions 1 and 2 have a contiguous relationship, and 0 otherwise. W is symmetric by construction and will have zeros on the main diagonal (i.e. a unit cannot be a "neighbour" of itself). There are a number of ways to construct W. Consider the following regular lattices:

Figure F.1. **Contiguity on a regular lattice**

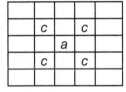

(a) Common Edge
(Rook case)

(b) Common Vertex
(Bishop case)

(c) Second Order
(Queen case)

Contiguity is here defined taking the example of a game of chess. In panel (a) contiguity is defined in relation to a shared border. In panel (b) contiguity is defined in terms of a common edge (or vertex). Panel (c) is a combination of (a) and (b) and also shows "second-order" contiguity (i.e. neighbourhood is defined in relation to the two closest units), as opposed to the "first-order" contiguity in (a) and (b). In practical applications, second-order and higher contiguity structures are rarely used. There are of course other ways to define contiguity (*e.g.* definitions that rely on the length of the common border), but these are the most common.

A transformation is often used to convert W to have row-sums of unity, giving a "standardised" version of the weight matrix. The motivation for standardisation can be seen by considering matrix multiplication of the standardised matrix C and a vector of observations y on a variable associated with the regions. This matrix product, $y^* = Cy$, thus represents a new variable equal to the mean of observations from contiguous regions. This is one way of quantifying the relationship $y_i = f(y_j)$, $j \neq i$. A simple linear relationship would be expressed as

$$y = \rho Cy + \varepsilon \tag{5}$$

where ρ is the (spatial) regression parameter to be estimated, measuring the average influence of neighbouring or contiguous observations. We could also calculate the proportion of total variation in y explained by spatial dependence using $\hat{\rho}Cy$, where $\hat{\rho}$ is the estimated value of ρ.

A fundamental principle that relates to spatial contiguity is the notion of a spatial lag operator, similar to the time-shift operators in time-series analysis. Thus, $D^p y_i = y_{i-p}$ is a pth order spatial lag. In applied situations, the concept of spatial lag relates to the set of neighbours associated with a particular location. That is, the lag works to produce a weighted average of the neighbouring observations. This avoids the problem of having to choose the direction of spatial dependence (*i.e.* there can be an infinite number of directional shifts and thus of parameters to be estimated).

Spatial weight matrices based on distance

Another way to construct spatial weight matrices for areal data is to use the geographical distance (linear distance or travel time distance, or a combination of the two) between two points (regions' centroids or other spatial units such as cities). There are two main types of distance matrices:

i) Distance band matrices, where a distance threshold is pre-set (for all spatial units) below which a region is considered as a neighbour.

The problem with this criterion is that it often leads to a very unbalanced connectedness structure. For example, this is the case when the spatial units have very different areas (as in the case of OECD regions), resulting in the smaller units having many neighbours, while the larger ones may have very few. A commonly used alternative is therefore:

ii) The k-nearest neighbours matrix, which computes a region-specific distance threshold so that each region has the same (pre-set) number of neighbours. In other words, no matter how distant one region is from other regions, each will have the same number of neighbours.

134

The guiding principle in selecting a definition for W should be the nature of the problem being studied, and perhaps additional non-sample information. However, in practice, the definition is often chosen *a priori*. In other words, we are often compelled to choose a spatial structure even before knowing how spatiality is structured. That is, we first choose W and then we use it to model the spatial structure, *i.e.* W is given, not estimated. This is obviously an undesirable feature because there is a risk of falling into a circular reasoning, in that the spatial structure, which the analyst may wish to discover in the data, has to be assumed known before data analysis is actually carried out. For this reason it is important to do a sensitivity analysis on the choice of the weight matrix.

Spatial models

Once we have chosen a spatial weight matrix, we can proceed to model estimation. Many of the models estimated are special cases of the following general autoregressive model:

$$y = \rho W_1 y + X\beta + u$$
$$u = \lambda W_2 u + \varepsilon \qquad (6)$$
$$\varepsilon \sim N(0, \sigma^2 I_n)$$

where y is an $n \times 1$ vector of dependent variables, X is an $n \times k$ matrix of explanatory variables, W_1 and W_2 are known $n \times n$ weight matrices, and I_n is the $n \times n$ identity matrix. From the general model (6) we can derive special models by imposing restrictions.

Setting $X = 0$ and $W_2 = 0$ we obtain a first-order spatial autoregressive model (FAR):

$$y = \rho W_1 y + \varepsilon \qquad (7)$$
$$\varepsilon \sim N(0, \sigma^2 I_n)$$

where W has been standardised and y is expressed in deviations-from-the-mean form to eliminate the constant term. This model attempts to explain variation in y as a linear combination of contiguous units with no other explanatory variable. It is therefore seldom used in applied work. Probably the most frequent use of the FAR model is in checking residuals for autocorrelation.

Setting $W_2 = 0$ produces a mixed regressive-spatial autoregressive (SAR) model:

$$y = \rho W_1 y + X\beta + \varepsilon \qquad (8)$$
$$\varepsilon \sim N(0, \sigma^2 I_n)$$

This model is analogous to the lagged dependent variable model in time series. This is the model that we use here.

Setting $W_1 = 0$ we obtain a regression model with spatial autocorrelation in the disturbances (SEM):

$$y = X\beta + u$$
$$u = \lambda W_2 u + \varepsilon \qquad\qquad (9)$$
$$\varepsilon \sim N(0, \sigma^2 I_n)$$

A related model is the Spatial Durbin Model (SDM), where a "spatial lag" of the dependent variable as well as a spatial lag of the explanatory variables are added to the traditional OLS model:

$$y = \rho W_1 y + X\beta_1 + W_1 X\beta_2 + \varepsilon \qquad\qquad (10)$$
$$\varepsilon \sim N(0, \sigma^2 I_n)$$

OECD PUBLISHING, 2, rue André-Pascal, 75775 PARIS CEDEX 16
PRINTED IN FRANCE
(04 2009 02 1 P) ISBN 978-92-64-03945-2 – No. 56701 2009

CPSIA information can be obtained at www.ICGtesting.com
Printed in the USA
BVOW06s1232260616

453463BV00003B/11/P